THE RULES OF ENGAGEMENT

If you live long enough
you will come across
a problem that
money, contacts, or
medicine cannot solve.
Only the knowledge of the
The Rules of Engagement
can save you.

★ ★

KAKRA BAIDEN
FOREWORD BY EASTWOOD ANABA

The Rules of Engagement
by Kakra Baiden

Printed in the United States of America

ISBN: 978-0-9968588-0-9

Scripture quotations are taken from the
King James Version of the Bible.

The author has added italics in Scripture
and text for emphasis.

E-mail: info@kakrabaiden.org

Dedication

To Rev. Herbert Armstrong Mensah.
Thank you for being my childhood friend.

Acknowledgments

My thanks and gratitude go to the following
for their help:

Yaw Amponsah-Baa, Eugene Gyawu, Brian Adu,
Sam Sawyerr, Kofi Asante, Edwin Moses,
Fifthson McApreku, Dr. Ben Abuaku,
John Opoku, Michael Adu-Opoku,
Josephine Gyawu, Helen Adu,
Faustina Armstrong Mensah,
and Afua Amponsah-Baa.

Contents

Foreword

by Rev. Eastwood Anaba

THERE IS OBVIOUSLY a prayer revival in many parts of the world. The results of the prayers are, however, not proportionate to the quantum of the prayers. The Church is praying much but with little results. The reason for this disparity can be traced to the fact that many believers don't know how to pray. Jesus' disciples knew that knowing how to pray determines the results of prayer so they asked Jesus how to pray.

And it came to pass, that, as he was praying in a certain place, when he ceased, one of his disciples said unto him, Lord, teach us to pray, as John also taught his disciples (Luke 11:1).

Believers who know how to pray don't necessarily obtain results that glorify God. They sometimes produce destructive outcomes of prayer because they pray amiss. Wrong motives and evil ambition make believers pray for results that gratify their lusts but have nothing to do with the Kingdom of God.

Ye lust, and have not: ye kill, and desire to have, and cannot obtain: ye fight and war, yet ye have not, because ye ask not. Ye ask, and receive not, because ye ask amiss, that ye may consume it upon your lusts (James 4:2-3).

It is in the light of the challenges I have mentioned above that Kakra Baiden's book, *The Rules of Engagement*, is relevant to our times. In this great work of revelation, the prophet instructs believers to pray strategically and earnestly. There is no substitute for experience, and the man of God demonstrates prayer with his personal experience. No one can write about prayer and make impact who does not pray. The keys to effective prayer are clearly laid out and the character of the praying person is evidently displayed.

Kakra Baiden is a man whose ministry is marked by signs and wonders. He states clearly that prayer is the key to his miracle ministry. As a sought-after apostle of the prophetic insight, he shows the way. Anybody who wishes to experience the miracle-working power of God has the right tool in their hands—this book—*The Rules of Engagement*.

And the lord commended the unjust steward, because he had done wisely: for the children of this world are in their generation wiser than the children of light (Luke 16:8).

The Rules of Engagement can be defined as the principles and practices that are adopted by a military outfit of organisations in situations of opposing interest in order to gain advantage. The military and secular organisations are serious about the rules of engagement. The Church is, however, largely indifferent, and the time to wake up is now.

Chapter 1

The Rules of Engagement

WHO HAS CHANGED, GOD OR ME?

OVER THE YEARS I have seen my prayer life improve and the power behind my prayer strengthen. Demons it took hours to cast out now come out in minutes. Answers to prayer that took days are now secured within minutes. I have seen God perform outstanding miracles through prayer.

By the grace of God I have seen God perform miracles that defy medical science. I have asked myself what has brought about this change in my prayer life. Has God changed or I have changed? Surely it couldn't be God, because in Malachi 3:6, He said, "I am the Lord and I change not."

If God cannot change, then I am the one who has changed. Something about me must have changed with the resultant change in my prayer life. I believe this change has come about because over time my understanding of the rules of engagement concerning prayer has increased. I would like to share with you a testimony someone sent to me after I prayed for her.

Healed of Sickling Status (AS)!

Dear Prophet,

I write to express my sincere appreciation and thanks to God Almighty for what He has done for me through you.

I have lived with sickle cell (AS) for twenty-four years with doctors restricting me from many things, especially cold or frozen foods. Any time I overlooked these warnings, I fell ill and experienced low BP.

One day I heard you preaching on one of the radio stations in my region where you read a testimony of a sickling patient who was healed. I felt pressed to call you because I believed I would be healed.

One day I called you whilst at a shopping mall. You picked up the call and asked for my request. To be honest, because the place was noisy I did not hear what you said in your prayer for me. All I heard was *"Amen!"*

When I came out of the mall my skin colour had changed into that of a newly born baby. Many looked at me in admiration, whilst others smiled at me. This was very rare to me.

Upon going through some tests afterwards, my report read AA. I was no longer AS. I have really received my healing! Thank you, Prophet, for allowing yourself for God to use you!

WHAT ARE THE RULES OF ENGAGEMENT?

The word "engagement" is usually related to marriage, but it also means a battle between two opposing armies. "Rules of engagement" means the rules that govern a battle or fight. Rules of engagement determine when soldiers are allowed to shoot during near-combat or combat conditions. For example, when the UN sends soldiers on peacekeeping missions, they are given the rules of their engagement.

The Rwandan Civil War

I recently watched a film about a massacre that took place during the Rwandan civil war. In the film, *Dogs of War*, which is based on a true story, hundreds of Tutsis were under the protection of UN forces on the compound of a Catholic church. Outside the compound were hundreds of Hutus, armed with machetes, knives, and guns.

In the course of the ensuing tensions, the soldiers received new rules of engagement. It was changed from peacekeeping to the evacuation of foreign nationals. After the evacuation, the vulnerable civilians were slaughtered by the armed Hutus. Only one person survived to tell the story. All of this happened because the soldiers had to follow the "rules of engagement."

WE ARE IN A BATTLE

For though we walk in the flesh, we do not *war* after the flesh: (For the weapons of our warfare are not carnal, but mighty through God to the pulling down of strong holds) (2 Cor. 10:3-4).

Whether or not you are aware, the Bible tells us that we are in a war. Our battle is not a physical one but a spiritual one, and our main enemy is the devil. God has also provided us with spiritual weapons to conduct this war. One of the principal weapons of a Christian is *prayer*.

PRAYER IS A WEAPON

Finally, my brethren, be strong in the Lord, and in the power of his might. Put on the whole *armour* of God, that ye may be able to stand against the wiles of the devil. For we wrestle not against flesh and blood, but against principalities, against powers, against the rulers of the darkness of this world, against spiritual wickedness in high places. Wherefore take unto you the whole armour of God, that ye may be able to withstand in the evil day, and having done all, to stand. . . . *praying always* with all prayer and supplication in the Spirit, and watching thereunto with all *perseverance* and *supplication* for all saints (Eph. 6:10-13, 18).

We are supposed to put on spiritual armour to fight the devil. This armour can be divided into two categories: *the defensive* and *the offensive.* Prayer is the main offensive weapon. I would like us to look more closely at verse 18, which highlights the offensive weapon called prayer.

First of all, we are to pray always. Then we are to pray with supplication. This means to plead for mercy. Then finally we are told to pray with perseverance. We must not give up on prayer. This is because it takes time for some prayers to be answered and it is sometimes not easy to pray for the saints, especially those you don't like.

My Experience with a Gun

To be able to use the weapon of prayer effectively you need to be trained by learning the rules of engagement. Some time ago someone offered to teach me how to shoot. He taught me basic rules of handling a gun effectively.

My prayers have become more effective and powerful than before because my understanding of the rules of prayer has improved over time. This has affected my prayer life tremendously and is the reason I can now pray more effectively.

A Deformed Leg Restored

One day I received a call from a church member whose wife had just delivered a baby girl with a deformed leg. The doctors and nurses had not broken the news to the mother as a result of this. The baby was still being kept in the nursery.

When I arrived, the anxious father took me to pray for the baby. After praying, the deformed leg remained the same. Nothing changed! I told the father not to worry because I believed God would heal the baby.

About an hour after we had left the ward, we heard screams. We went back into the ward to find that the deformed leg had been replaced by a perfect, brand new leg.

I remember when I woke up the following day; it was as though I had been dreaming. However, it was real. I saw the power of God! This tells you the power of prayer.

TEACH US TO PRAY

The Prayer Life of Jesus

Jesus had a powerful and effective prayer life. He was found praying many times in the Bible.

And in the morning, rising up a great while before day, he went out, and departed into a solitary place, and there *prayed* (Mark 1:35).

And it came to pass in those days, that he went out into a mountain to *pray*, and continued all night in prayer to God (Luke 6:12).

Now when all the people were baptized, it came to pass, that Jesus also being baptized, and *praying*, the heaven was opened, And the Holy Ghost descended in a bodily shape like a dove upon him, and a voice came from heaven, which said, Thou art my beloved Son; in thee I am well pleased (Luke 3:21-22).

Any time Jesus prayed, there were serious results. The disciples said to each other,

What manner of man is this! for he commandeth even the winds and water, and they obey him (Luke 8:25b).

In other words, they said, "Why is this man's prayer different from ours? We all pray, but He seems to have answers to prayer."

Why Is It That We Could Not Cast Him Out?

In Matthew 17, a man whose son was suffering from epilepsy was brought to the disciples for prayer, but they could not heal him. Later, when he was brought to Jesus, He . . .

. . . rebuked the devil; and he departed out of him: and the child was cured from that very hour (Matt. 17:18).

His disciples asked, "Why is it that we could not cast him out?"

Why is the prayer of some people more potent than others? Why is it that sometimes when you pray you don't have any results, but when someone else prays for you over the same issue there are results?

One day, the disciples of Jesus approached Him concerning their ineffective prayers. Luke 11:1 states, "It came to pass, that, as he was praying in a certain place, when he ceased, one of his disciples said unto him, Lord, *teach us to pray*, as John also taught his disciples."

They had come to the realization that the mere act of praying was not sufficient for answered prayer. Effective prayer had to be based on knowledge and they needed to be taught the "rules of engagement." Because of this they decided to go for "further studies." They said, "Teach us to pray." They must have wondered what made Him get all those results.

What made the prayer life of Jesus so powerful? It is simple! He understood the "rules of engagement."

Chapter 2

Understanding the Rules of Engagement

He that turneth away his ear from *hearing the law*, even his prayer shall be abomination (Prov. 28:9).

THE WORD "LAW" MEANS RULES, and the word "abomination" means disgusting. I would like to rephrase this verse to make the meaning clearer. "Prayer is based on laws or rules and the man who does not observe these laws will pray all right, but it will be disgusting before the Lord."

There are many who think the mere fact that they are praying means God is listening to their prayers. The mere act of praying does not guarantee answered prayer. Answered prayer is based on knowledge of the rules of engagement.

Matthew chapter 6 is one of my favourite passages in the Bible. In it, Jesus taught extensively about prayer. I want us to examine some of the things He said concerning prayer.

MISCONCEPTIONS ABOUT PRAYER

And when thou prayest, thou shalt not be as the hypocrites [are]: for they love to pray standing in the synagogues and in the corners of the streets, that they may be seen of men. Verily I say unto you, They have their reward. But thou, when thou prayest, enter into thy closet, and when thou hast shut thy door, pray to thy Father which is in secret; and thy Father which seeth in secret shall reward thee openly. But when ye pray, use not vain repetitions, as the heathen [do]: for they think that they shall be heard for their much speaking.

Be not ye therefore like unto them: for your Father knoweth what things ye have need of, before ye ask him (Matt. 6:5-7).

Matthew 6 generally deals with the subject of prayer. The first section largely deals with misconceptions about prayer. "Misconception" simply means something that is not properly understood. Here are a few misconceptions about prayer.

Answered Prayer Is Not Based on Your Geographical Location

...they love to pray in the *synagogues* and the *corners of the streets* (Matt. 6:5).

The Pharisees loved to pray in specific places: the synagogues and the corners of the streets. To them, location was a big part of their prayer life. One day I tried to make an appointment with an evangelist friend of mine to discuss certain issues. When I asked him where he would be that weekend, he answered, "I will not be around this week. I am going for a retreat at so-and-so mountains to pray." This gentleman, however, made a comment that had me very worried. He said, "When I don't pray on that mountain, God does not hear my prayers."

There are people who believe that unless they pray at particular locations, God will not hear their prayers. It could be a church building, a field, a room, or a place where they may have had some special or supernatural experience. They seem to have faith only when they pray in these special locations. The temptation to recapture and immortalize spiritual experiences becomes very strong.

If you will remember, when Jesus was transfigured, Peter, James, and John suggested that three booths be built so that they remain at that place. They wanted to make that spiritual experience permanent. In fact, there are many pastors who do not have much faith when they pray outside their church building. They will often ask you to come to their church for prayer because their faith is very low.

Imagine you have a gun that only works in your house. A real gun should be able to work in all locations: on the street, in the kitchen, in a mall, and even in the bathroom. That is what makes it a real weapon. If it does not, then it is not a proper gun.

Jesus prayed everywhere: on the mountain, at sea, at a wedding, on the streets, people's homes, and while walking on the road. In fact, many of Jesus' miracles occurred outside the church. Do you know why? It was because He knew that answered prayer is not based on a geographical location.

When your prayer is based on a geographical location you limit the power of God. That is why I pray for people anywhere and everywhere. I have seen fantastic miracles over the telephone, through the Internet, etc.

Sickler Healed

One day I prayed over the phone for someone who was sickling positive. I asked her to do a medical examination after the prayer. Later she went to conduct a test and the results proved that she had become sickling negative. There were many things that could have undermined my faith.

One, it is medically impossible for a sickling positive person to become sickling negative. I thank God that it is medically impossible, but with God, all things are possible.

Two, I prayed from my bedroom.

Three, I could not see her because she was not physically present.

You Can Pray Powerfully at Meal Times

Do you know that you can pray powerfully even in the middle of a meal? Even a restaurant cannot stop the power of prayer. You can eat, pause, pray, and continue eating.

Jesus was having supper with His disciples when He taught an important subject like communion. He stopped in the middle of His supper, prayed, and continued eating.

And as they were eating, Jesus took bread, and blessed [it], and brake [it], and gave [it] to the disciples, and said, Take, eat; this is my body (Matt. 26:26).

One day someone called me from South Africa for prayer. After praying, the line went dead. After some seconds I heard the voice again. When I asked the person why there was a break, she answered, "I fell under the power."

The power of God went through the phone and knocked her over. All this happened while I was eating in my dining room. May you perform miracles while you are eating!

The Woman at the Well

In John 4 the Bible talks about a woman Jesus engaged in a conversation. She is commonly known as "the woman at the well." I want us to examine part of the conversation she had with Jesus. The woman said,

Our fathers worshipped in this mountain; and ye say, that in Jerusalem is the place where men ought to worship. Jesus saith unto her, Woman, believe me, the hour cometh, when ye shall neither in this mountain, nor yet at Jerusalem, worship the Father (John 4:20-21).

In other words, she said, "From my grandfather to my dad, we have always prayed on that mountain." Her whole faith and prayer life were based on a geographical location. In essence she was saying, "Until I pray on that mountaintop, God will not hear me." Jesus said, "Ye worship *ye know not what*: we know what we worship: for salvation is of the Jews" (John 4:22).

Why was this woman relying on location to receive answered prayer? The answer is simple! Pure ignorance! Jesus said, "Ye know not what." In other words, you are ignorant about the "rules of engagement." Whether you are in a five-star hotel or a prison, God can still hear your prayer. Jesus continued,

But the hour cometh, and now is, when the true worshippers shall worship the Father in *spirit* and in *truth*: for the Father seeketh such to worship him (John 4:23).

Prayer is driven by *truth*, the principles of the *Word of God,* and *the leading of the Spirit.* That is what makes prayer effective.

Answered Prayer Is Not Necessarily Based on Lengthy Prayers

But when ye pray, use not vain repetitions, as the heathen [do]: for they think that they shall be heard for their *much speaking* (Matt. 6:7).

There are people who think "much speaking" or long prayer is the solution to answered prayer. This is not entirely true. I am not saying long prayers are not important. I personally believe in praying for a long time. Just today I have prayed for five hours. There are even times when I have prayed for days. However, praying for a long time does not necessarily mean your prayers are going to be answered.

Lengthy prayer is and can be necessary, but it does not necessarily guarantee answered prayer. Jesus Himself used to pray for long periods of time.

And in the morning, rising up a great while before day, he went out, and departed into a solitary place, and there prayed (Mark 1:35).

And it came to pass in those days, that he went out into a mountain to pray, and continued all night in prayer to God (Luke 6:12).

But He was the same person who said long prayers do not necessarily mean answered prayers.

There are people who assume that because they have been for an all-night prayer meeting it means their prayers have been answered. They become frustrated when they do not see any results. Nothing could be further from the truth.

A student who requests more paper during an exam but has not studied for it will still fail, irrespective of how many sheets he collects. It will be just a waste of his time. All that extra paper will not make any difference.

As my knowledge about prayer has increased, I have noticed that my public prayers have become shorter and more powerful. When I am alone in my closet talking to God, I usually pray for long, but publicly, I pray for a short time.

The prophets of Baal cried all day but their prayers were unanswered. Elijah just prayed for a minute and fire fell from heaven. His prayers were answered.

Sometimes empty heads and hearts who may not have even read their Bibles the whole year assume that the passage of time alone guarantees answered prayer. Many people who are like that unfortunately have very little success in prayer.

In the book of Isaiah the Bible records God's response to the lengthy prayers of Israel, "And when ye spread forth your hands, I will hide mine eyes from you: yea, when ye make many prayers, I will not hear: your hands are full of blood" (Isa.1:15). They made "many prayers," thinking it would bring them answers, but God told them to "Learn to do well..." (Isa. 1:17).

Their problem was ignorance; they had not learned the "rules of engagement."

The Woman Who Suffered from Schizophrenia

One day I received a call from one of my pastors who said that a certain woman suffering from schizophrenia had been brought to the church for prayer. We were supposed to have an all-night prayer meeting that day. I told him to organize some of the pastors to pray for her but he insisted they wait for me. I decided to rest for a while before going for the all-night prayer meeting.

In my sleep, the Lord appeared to me and said, "Effective prayer is not just based on how long you pray. When you meet that sick woman, do not pray for more than one minute or I will not listen to your prayers. Just command the spirit to leave and I will do it."

Later when I got to the church I met the woman and her family waiting anxiously for me. I laid my hands on her and said, "In the name of Jesus, I release you from any demonic power that hinders your mind. Amen!" I turned to her family members and announced, "She is healed!"

They looked at me in disbelief and asked, "Ah, Pastor, is that all?" I could tell from their faces that they were confused. Why? Because they had associated effective prayer with long prayers.

I asked them, "Should I test her to find out if she has become normal?" They said yes. I started chatting with her and she answered all my questions intelligently; she was normal! They still could not believe because their problem was it could not be that fast. I told them to bring her back to the church after one week. "You will come and testify to me that she is normal," I added.

They called me after three days with joy and told me they had observed her for the past three days and she had truly been healed. The following Sunday when I came to church I saw some people dressed in white. I was told that it was the family of the woman who had come to give thanks to the Lord. She had been completely healed! Praise God!

That is why I do not pray for long when I am about to eat. After all, only two words, "Come out," brought Lazarus out of the dead. How long do you think I should pray over a plate of rice and chicken? I just say, "Thank You," and that's all. From today you are going to pray like that, in the name of Jesus!

The Prayer of the Pharisees

Which devour widows' houses, and for a shew *make long prayers*: the same shall receive greater damnation (Luke 20:47).

The Pharisees prayed for long but did not cast out demons, heal the sick, perform miracles, or even raise a mosquito. In summary, they had a very ineffective prayer life irrespective of their long prayers.

Answered Prayer Is Not Based on the Volume of Your Voice

Whether you pray loudly or silently has no bearing on answered prayer unless it is by the influence of the Holy Spirit. Some people equate power in prayer with the volume of their voice. God is neither deaf nor nervous. Hebrews 5:7 describes the prayer of Jesus in the garden of Gethsemane:

Who in the days of his flesh, when he had offered up prayers and supplications with *strong crying* and *tears* unto him that was able to save him from death, and was *heard* in that he *feared* (Heb. 5:7).

The most intense prayer of Jesus was in the garden of Gethsemane. Many people quote this verse to support loud prayers. However, I would like to point out that Jesus was not heard because of the tears, strong crying, or sweat. He was "heard in that *He feared.*" The fear of God was one of the secrets to His powerful prayer life—not the volume of His voice.

Another Scripture that is used to support shouting is Romans 8:26, which says,

Likewise the Spirit also helpeth our infirmities: for we know not what we should pray for as we ought: but the Spirit itself maketh intercession for us with *groanings which cannot be uttered* (Rom. 8:26).

This Scripture rather supports silent prayer, because remember, they are *groanings which cannot be uttered or spoken*. If we can hear it, then it cannot be groaning which cannot be uttered.

You can scream or whisper the whole night, but if you don't fear God, you cannot have the results that Jesus had in prayer. When you go for an all-night prayer meeting, remember, your sweating and screaming does not necessarily mean your prayers are being answered. Similarly, if you sit silently like a monk, it also does not mean that God will answer your prayers. Whether your prayers are answered or not will be based on the rules of engagement and the leading of the Spirit.

Personally, I do not have a problem with either shouting or whispering because I do both; sometimes I shout, and sometimes I am silent by the leading of the Spirit.

Silent Prayer Can Produce Results

Hannah prayed to God for a child and because there was no sound, Eli thought Hannah was drunk. Regardless of the silence, it was a prayer that moved heaven.

Now Hannah, she *spake in her heart*; only *her lips moved*, but *her voice was not heard*: therefore Eli thought she had been drunken (1 Sam. 1:13).

Eli, who probably equated powerful prayer with shouting, thought Hannah was drunk and despised her, but her silent prayer produced results.

Loud Prayer Can Produce Results

And when he thus had spoken, he cried with *a loud voice*, Lazarus, come forth. And he that was dead came forth, bound hand and foot with graveclothes: and his face was bound about with a napkin. Jesus saith unto them, Loose him, and let him go (John 11:43-44).

At the raising of Lazarus, Jesus raised His voice and commanded the dead man to come out and Lazarus was instantly raised from the dead. There is a place for shouting in prayer and shouting can sometimes raise the dead. Amen!

In my own experience I have frequently shouted and commanded evil spirits to come out of people. Shouting or whispering is only powerful if it is by the leading of the Spirit.

Answered Prayer Is Not Entirely Based on Fasting

Moreover when ye *fast*, be not, as the hypocrites, of a sad countenance: for they disfigure their faces, that they may appear unto men to fast. Verily I say unto you, They have their reward (Matt. 6:16).

Fasting is very good, but it must be governed by the rules of engagement. Many fast but are not aware that they are actually on a hunger strike. The fact that you are hungry does not mean God will answer your prayers. On the other hand, when you fast and follow the rules of engagement, God will answer your prayers.

Jesus said the prayers and fasting of the Pharisees were impotent because of their disregard for the rules of engagement. Isaiah 58 talks about a group who fasted for some time but still had no answer. They went to God and demanded a reason for the silence in heaven. They said, "Wherefore have we fasted, [say they], and thou seest not? [wherefore] have we afflicted our soul, and thou takest no knowledge? (Isa. 58:3-4).

They made the dangerous assumption that once they were on a fast, their prayers were getting to heaven. If it was so, then God would have to answer the prayer of witches who are on a fast!

God replied, "Behold, in the day of your fast ye find pleasure, and exact all your labours. Behold, ye fast for strife and debate, and to smite with the fist of wickedness: ye shall not fast as [ye do this] day, to make your voice to be heard on high" (Isa. 58:3-4).

God said, "This type of fast cannot secure answers, because fasting has to be based on the rules of engagement."

He Is Supposed to Divorce His Wife and Marry Me

One day a certain lady told me someone's husband was supposed to marry her. Therefore she was embarking on a fast. When I asked her why, she said, "I had a vision where God showed me that his previous marriage was only registered on earth, but not in heaven. Therefore, heaven did not accept the marriage."

"What is supposed to happen?" I asked her. She replied, "He is supposed to divorce his wife and marry me." I was amazed!

There are some who hatch wicked plans and try to force God to endorse them through fasting and prayer. They have the belief that God will answer their prayers once they are fasting. It is a misconception! God will only hear your prayers when they are based on the rules of engagement. After reading this book, may you receive answers to your prayers!

Chapter 3

The Rule of Relationships

FATHER-SON RELATIONSHIP

ANSWERED PRAYER IS DETERMINED BY the law of relationships. One day a certain young woman told me how she had given her ex-boyfriend thousands of dollars as a loan without collateral or a receipt. She did not hesitate to do it because she was deeply in love. When the relationship ended, she could not retrieve her money since there was no evidence. She was ready and willing to part with her savings because of the relationship that existed between them.

That is why you must be careful who you love because the deeper the relationship you have with someone, the more vulnerable you become to the person. Song of Solomon 8:7 describes the power of a love relationship.

Many waters cannot quench love, neither can the floods drown it: if a man would *give* all the substance of his house for love, it would utterly be contemned (Song of Solomon 8:7).

This Scripture was made real to me when a brother I knew made a woman he had just met a joint owner of his company. He was a smart businessman, but love made him "stupid." The relationship was short lived and he had to face the consequences of a fatal attraction.

You can ask Samson about the rule of relationships. He revealed the secret of his strength to Delilah, an agent of his enemies, and it cost him his life. Love can make you give all the substance of your house. I have seen hardcore businessmen and women transform into "zombies" when they fall in love. I have seen them ripped off as they have handed over huge sums of money because they were "high on love."

THE FOUNDATION OF
ANSWERED PRAYER

In Matthew 6:9, Jesus taught that the foundation or bedrock of answered prayer is our *relationship* with God.

After this manner therefore pray ye: *Our Father* which art in heaven, Hallowed be thy name. Thy kingdom come (Matt. 6:9-10a).

Jesus said when you pray, say, "*our Father.*" The word "father" represents the highest relationship.

Our relationship with God is the foundation on which all prayer rests. All the promises in the

Lord's Prayer, like, "Give us our daily bread," and "Deliver us from evil," are all determined by this relationship; the father-son relationship.

The Prodigal Son

In the story of the prodigal son, the younger son was bold enough to ask for half of his father's estate. Luke 15:11-12 reads, "And he said, A certain man had two sons: And the younger of them said to his father, *Father, give me the portion of goods that falleth to me*. And he divided unto them his living."

Why is it that the hardworking servants could not ask for half of their master's estate? Very simple! A master-servant relationship is a lower form of relationship. It is lower than a father-son relationship. A master-servant relationship entitles you to daily wages or a salary, but a father-son relationship entitles you to an inheritance; everything!

Good Gifts Are for Children

The same law can be found in the words of Jesus in the book of Luke. Luke 11:9-13 reads,

And I say unto you, Ask, and it shall be given you; seek, and ye shall find; knock, and it shall be opened unto you. For every one that asketh receiveth; and he that seeketh findeth; and to him that knocketh it shall be opened. If a *son* shall ask bread of any of you that is a *father*, will he give him a stone? or if he ask a fish, will he for a fish give him a serpent? Or if he shall ask an egg, will he offer him a scorpion? If ye then, being evil, know how to give good gifts unto your *children*: how much more shall your heavenly *Father* give the Holy Spirit to them that ask him?

Men at Work!

One day whilst driving my daughter home from school I came across a beggar by the road-side, hoping to receive some tips from the passing motorists. Some people totally ignored him and others threw coins at him.

When I passed by him, I gave him some money. Before we got home, my daughter said in her sweet little voice, "Daddy, I want you to buy me some sweets." I drove to a nearby shop and bought her sweets, plus other things she had not asked for.

My daughter did not need to beg or work for the sweets because of the relationship that exists between us. She is my darling daughter and I am her daddy, period! I was willing to do exceedingly and abundantly above all that she could ask for or even think of.

If you want to have an effective prayer life, the first thing you must do is make God your father by repenting. This will establish a father-son relationship and change your prayer life. Many people seek to be religious instead of developing a good relationship with God. I believe the power of your prayer life is largely determined by the quality of your relationship with God.

A Good Relationship Counts

And he that sent me is with me: the *Father* hath not left me alone; for I do always those things that please him (John 8:29).

Deprived of a Father's Inheritance

Someone once told me the story of a very wealthy man who died and left his only son nothing. Instead he gave his wealth to people who were not his blood relations. When I asked why, I was told that he had a very bad relationship with his son.

There are children of God who have a very bad relationship with their heavenly Father. This tends to rob them of their inheritance in Christ. Some Christians have unanswered prayers because of the bad relationship they have with their heavenly Father.

A life of sin can seriously damage your relationship with God. The story of the prodigal son reminds me of the consequences of having a bad relationship with your heavenly Father. It cuts your prayer or communication links and deprives you of the blessings of God. The story of the prodigal son goes like this:

And he said, A certain man had two sons: And the younger of them said to his father, Father, give me the portion of goods that falleth to me. And he divided unto them his living. And not many days after the younger son gathered all together, and took his journey into a far country, and there wasted his substance with *riotous living*. And when he had spent all, there arose a mighty famine in that land; and he began to be in want (Luke 15:11-14).

This story describes the relationship between a rebellious son and his father. The result of the son's rebellion was separation, sin, and finally, hardships. The communication between father and son was cut because "he went to a far country." Sin will always sever the communication lines, or prayer, between you and your heavenly Father.

Sometimes when it is raining and the clouds are very dark and heavy, my TV decoder goes off and I receive a message, "no signal." It always reminds me of Isaiah 44:22: "I have blotted out, as a *thick cloud*, thy transgressions, and, as a cloud, thy sins: return unto me; for I have redeemed thee." In these verses, God compares the sins of Israel with clouds, which obscure the face of the sun. Walk righteously before God so you don't receive a message from heaven which says, "no signal."

Later, the son repented, restored the relationship, and started communicating or praying to his father again. The result was a restoration of what he had lost because of the father's mercy. The story ends like this:

And the son said unto him, Father, I have sinned against heaven, and in thy sight, and am no more worthy to be called thy son. But the father said to his servants, Bring forth the best robe, and put it on him; and put a ring on his hand, and shoes on his feet: And bring hither the fatted calf, and kill it; and let us eat, and be merry: For this my son was dead, and is alive again; he was lost, and is found. And they began to be merry (Luke 15:21-24).

To have an effective prayer life, your primary concern must be to develop a very good personal relationship with God, because sin separates us from God and makes Him not hear your voice.

Isaiah 59:1-2 says, "Behold, the Lord's hand is not shortened, that it cannot save; neither his ear heavy, that it cannot hear: But your iniquities have separated between you and your God, and your sins have hid his face from you, that he will not hear."

The Unscrupulous Businessman

Years ago I visited the workshop of a businessman who was supposed to manufacture some furniture for us. We had already pre-financed it. I was told he was on a twenty-one-day fast, so I could not see him. I said, "This man must be a very spiritual person." Later I came to discover that he was a first-class liar and cheat because he tried to swindle us. I started wondering, "How can someone who prays and fasts for twenty-one days be so dishonest and such a big liar?"

Obviously he did not understand the rules of engagement; that a good relationship with God is more important than extended periods of fasting and prayer, because apart from separation, sin can act like a cloud, obscuring our communication with God.

The Rule of Relationships Raised the Dead

I don't know if you are familiar with the story of Lazarus. He had been dead for four days, but Jesus raised him from the dead.

Said I not unto thee, that, if thou wouldest believe, thou shouldest see the glory of God? Then they took away the stone [from the place] where the dead was laid. And Jesus lifted up [his] eyes, and said, *Father*, I thank thee that thou hast heard me (John 11:40-41).

The faith and confidence of Jesus that the dead man would be raised was drawn from the law of relationships. Jesus lifted up His eyes to heaven and said, "Father." He reminded Him of their relationship. He drew on His relationship with God to raise Lazarus.

I want to describe to you how I always picture it. I can see Him saying something like, "Daddy, this is Your Son, Jesus, the beloved one; not the stubborn one, but the one in whom You are well pleased. Your Son needs a favour. I have this dead friend who will not wake up. Please raise him up for Me."

I am sure God looked into His eyes and said something like, "That's my darling boy. Ooh, I love Him. 'Okay Son, I will raise him up. Your prayer is My delight.'"

It reminds me of my own little daughter, Chloe. When she lifts up those cute eyes to look into my eyes and says, "Daddy, I need an ice cream," something just breaks in my heart. When my kids ask me for something legitimate, I find it hard to say no! The moment I hear that magical word, "Daddy," they charm me. They rely on the power of relationships to get me to answer their prayer, not hard work.

Jesus continued,

And I knew that thou hearest me always: but because of the people which stand by I said [it], that they may believe that thou hast sent me. And when he thus had spoken, *he cried with a loud voice*, Lazarus, come forth (John 11:42-43).

It is important to notice the order of events. The foundation of the prayer was the magical word "Father," then came the prayer, and then came the shouting, "Lazarus, come out!" The relationship came before shouting. Without the relationship, you can shout, but it will be in vain.

I can employ someone to work for me, clean my house, etc., but he can never be put on the same level with my children. Why? Because of the relationship I have with them!

The Rule of Relationships Opens the Heavens

Now when all the people were baptized, it came to pass, that Jesus also being baptized, and praying, the heaven was opened, And the Holy Ghost descended in a bodily shape like a dove upon him, and a voice came from heaven, which said, Thou art my beloved Son; in thee I am well pleased (Luke 3:21-22).

Every time the heavens are opened, signs and wonders follow as heaven makes tangible contact with the earth. The baptism of Jesus was an awesome experience because the heavens opened and God spoke audibly concerning His Son.

The Heavens Opened Over My Life

I remember once praying and fasting for some days and seeking the fellowship of the Holy Spirit. On the fifth day of my fast, around three in the morning, I heard an audible voice call my name three times in the room: "Kakra, Kakra, Kakra." I shouted with joy, "Holy Spirit!" That day, the heavens had opened over my life. It was one of the most joyous experiences of my life.

In another instance I once went to pray on top of my father's house. It was covered with a concrete roof, which we used to use as sort of a huge balcony. On this particular day I woke up around 3 a.m. to pray. As soon as I started praying I felt a very strong presence that seemed to be building up. I turned and ran.

When I got to the door I could not open it. Not because the door was jammed, but because at that point, flesh was rebelling against command. My brain was sending a signal to my mind, "Open the door," but it refused. I turned round in fear to face whatever seemed to be coming. Then I saw the most amazing sight. I saw the heavens literally open and I saw Jesus coming from the skies. He was laughing as He descended and the whole world shook with His presence. It was during that experience that I received my call to the ministry.

The reason God manifested Himself at the baptism of Jesus was because of the law of relationships. He said, "This is my beloved Son." It was not primarily because of the fasting, prayer, or even the baptism. It was because of sonship.

Up until this point Jesus had not fasted for forty days. He had not started preaching, He had not even won one soul, but already His Father opened the heavens for Him. The reason was simple: the law of relationships!

Dear reader, if you want to develop a good prayer life your primary aim must be to develop a good, vibrant, healthy, and stable relationship with God. The heavens will open over your head and signs and wonders will follow.

RELATIONSHIP WITH
FELLOW HUMANS

Apart from our relationship with Christ, our relationship with fellow humans also greatly influences prayer. I would like us to examine three of these relationships.

1. The Relationship Between You and Your Spouse

That Your Prayers Be Not Hindered

Likewise, ye husbands, dwell with them according to knowledge, giving honour unto the wife, as unto the weaker vessel, and as being *heirs together* of the grace of life; that your *prayers be not hindered*. Finally, be ye all of one mind, having compassion one of another, love as brethren, be pitiful, be courteous: Not rendering evil for evil, or railing for railing: but contrariwise blessing; knowing that ye are thereunto called, that ye should inherit a blessing. For he that will love life, and see good days, let him refrain his tongue from evil, and his lips that they speak no guile:

Let him eschew evil, and do good; let him seek peace, and ensue it. For the eyes of the Lord are over the righteous, and his ears are open unto their prayers: but the face of the Lord is against them that do evil (1 Peter 3:7-12).

Husbands are supposed to dwell with their wives according to knowledge. What specific knowledge is this? It is the knowledge that without a good relationship with your spouse, your prayers will be hindered. It is amazing how God places great emphasis on relationships and prayer.

I have not come across any Scripture that expressly says, "If you do not give an offering or go for an all-night prayer meeting or pray for three hours, your prayers will be hindered." However, there is a Scripture that expressly says, "If you do not have a good relationship with your spouse, your prayers will be hindered."

If you understand this simple key, for the sake of enlightened self-interest, you will strive to have a good relationship with your spouse.

JOINT SIGNATORIES

My wife and I keep our money together. We are joint signatories to the same accounts. She can sign on the account and so can I. This level of financial cooperation has been achieved because of the level of relationship that exists between us.

It is a relationship of love, security, trust, and integrity. If I do not maintain a good relationship with my wife, the access I have to her accounts will be stopped. The relationship determines the level of access. In marriage, you become a joint signatory with your partner to a "joint spiritual account" that has been created in heaven for you. There is a bank in heaven that supplies our needs when we pray.

Philippians 4:19 says, "But my God shall supply all your need according to his riches in glory by Christ Jesus." Our needs, like spiritual gifts, healing, money, grace, babies, shoes, and houses, are all catered for by this account. The interesting thing to note here is that to access this account you will need the signature of your spouse, who is your co-signatory to the account. The signature is "a good relationship." For you to draw on this account you will need your spouse to countersign, otherwise the cheque cannot be cashed. Your prayers will be hindered.

It is interesting how you can have pastors who are quarrelling with their wives praying fervently on Saturday night concerning their Sunday morning service. I don't think God is impressed when He sees that because they have broken the law of relationship.

Sometimes pastors tend to think that because they have enjoyed success in ministry it puts them above the law, but remember that God is not a respecter of persons.

God Started Laughing

I remember once having a serious disagreement with my wife. Out of anger I went into my study to pray and wait on the Lord. When I began praying, it was as if I could hear God laughing. The Holy Spirit said to me, "Don't waste your time. Reconcile with your wife before you talk to Me." Knowing the rules of engagement, I quickly went to resolve the issue with my wife before I returned to my closet to continue praying, but this time with confidence.

It's funny, but sometimes in a marital relationship spouses become "spiritual" when there is strife in the house. That is when they camouflage strife with all sorts of worship songs like, "I Am Trading My Sorrows." Just shut up, swallow your pride, apologize, reconcile, and then let's have real worship.

Why Should Married People Love As Brethren?

First Peter 3:8 says, "Finally, [be ye] all of one mind, having compassion one of another, *love as brethren*, [be] pitiful, [be] courteous." If you have noticed, men are less sensitive and less prone to strife than women. One reason is because as "brothers" their threshold of tolerance is very high as compared to women. For marriage to be stressful and tension free, there is the need for brotherly love to continue.

Some people are so sensitive to the extent that you cannot even share a joke with them. When we are brothers, we can tease ourselves, we can laugh, we can joke, etc. It helps to free your heart from unforgiveness and bitterness. If you are too sensitive, you will always have a problem.

The Camouflage of Railing

First Peter 3:9 continues,

Not rendering evil for evil, or for *railing*: but contrariwise blessing; knowing that ye are thereunto called, that ye should inherit a blessing.

The word "railing" means to speak in a loud, abusive language. There are some issues in certain marriages that cannot be resolved. It could be about finance, in-laws, or a close relationship with someone of the opposite sex. As soon as one partner raises the subject, the other may begin to shout, scream, threaten, and sometimes cry. This attitude derails any logical and sincere conversation. In so doing, that area remains an unresolved issue of hurt, bitterness, frustration, and anger.

Some people go into history and begin screaming or crying about historical events that have no bearing on the current issues. They may say something like, "Last year, you forgot my birthday. You don't love me or care for me. I have wasted my time on you...." Meanwhile, the issue being discussed may be how the other partner misused money.

Come on, give me a break! Let's talk about the real issues! For the sake of their prayer lives, married couples should try to overcome this stumbling block and be able to discuss issues dispassionately to resolve them.

Do You Want to See Good Days?

First Peter 3:10-11 continues, "For he that will love life, and *see good days*, let him refrain his tongue from evil, and his lips that they speak no guile: Let him eschew evil, and do good; let him seek peace, and ensue it."

Prayer is a vehicle that helps you experience good days. It is a channel through which God provides for you and blesses you. It can bring financial, emotional, spiritual, and all kinds of blessings.

Many Christians are not seeing good days because their prayers are hindered. The same tongue that is used to praise God is used to insult at home. You will not see good days this way because your prayer will be hindered.

The Final Conclusion

Finally, Peter concludes by saying, "For the eyes of the Lord [are] over the righteous and his ears [*are open*] *unto their prayers*: but the face of the Lord [is] against them that do evil" (1 Peter 3:12). God is watching your relationship with your spouse more than your sanctimonious prayers in the church.

This verse summarizes all that has been said in the preceding verses. God is not happy with us when we live in marital disharmony. You may be hailed outside the walls of your home as a hero, but God's face will be against you. When you live in harmony with your spouse, God will even strain His ear to hear what you say in prayer.

If you hold something against your spouse, it is time to let it go because greater issues are at stake; your whole prayer life is at stake. Remember, the one who is able to seek peace is the one God is pleased with. That person will also have his prayers answered.

2. Your Relationship between Your Fellow Brothers and Sisters in Christ

Therefore if thou bring thy gift to the altar, and there rememberest that *thy brother hath ought against thee*; *leave* there thy gift before the altar, and *go* thy way; first be *reconciled to thy brother*, and then come and offer thy gift. Agree with thine adversary quickly, whiles thou art in the way with him; lest at any time the adversary deliver thee to the judge, and the judge deliver thee to the officer, and thou be cast into prison (Matt. 5:23-25).

This Scripture talks about how to give an offering as a gift to God. It could be an offering of money, praise, or worship.

A religious person may assume that his presence in church and his offering is enough to grant him audience with God and subsequently answered prayers. This is not true, because we are told that God values relationships between fellow believers more than prayer and offerings.

I like the phrase, "Leave there thy gift before the altar, and go thy way; be reconciled to thy brother and then come and offer thy gift." I once jokingly said, "God did not say take the gift away." He said, "Leave it at the altar, because maybe the pastor will like it, but I have rejected it until you reconcile with your brother."

There are many people giving to churches but not to God. They have many grudges with their fellow brothers and sisters yet still give offerings to God. God's verdict is final; He will reject it if you have something against your brother.

THE EXAMPLE OF JESUS

During Jesus' last days on earth, He retained a cordial relationship with His disciples, even Judas, although He knew they were going to betray Him. He did not harbour any bitterness or grudges against them. John 13:1-2 reads,

Now before the feast of the passover, when Jesus knew that his hour was come that he should depart out of this world unto the Father, *having loved his own which were in the world, he loved them unto the end.* And supper being ended, the devil having now put into the heart of Judas Iscariot, Simon's son, to betray him.

If I were in Jesus' shoes, I am sure I would have prayed against them saying, "May the earth open up and swallow them, may they be fatherless, etc." Jesus knew a good relationship with other believers is the key to experiencing answered prayer. Even on the cross, He prayed concerning His enemies and said, "Father, forgive them, for they know not what they do." He understood the "rules of engagement."

No wonder Hebrews 5:7-8 says, "Who in the days of his flesh, when he had offered up prayers and supplications with strong crying and tears unto him that was able to save him from death, and was heard in that he feared; Though he were a Son, yet learned he obedience by the things which he suffered."

Some prayer meetings are filled with people who are praying for their fellow believers and enemies to die. While our Saviour was praying for His enemies who took His life to live, we are praying for people who took our money to die;

and the most interesting part is the money is not even a lot.

Vision of Unforgiveness

One day I had a misunderstanding with a fellow Christian brother, and like we sometimes do, I said to myself, *I have forgiven him, but I will not have anything to do with him.* That night I had a very vivid vision that showed my spiritual condition.

I had been imprisoned with very hardened criminals and I was shocked that I, "a man of God," had been jailed with such company. I immediately started banging on the bars and screaming, "I am a pastor. I have done no wrong and I don't deserve to be locked up with hardened criminals." Eventually an angel appeared and said, "We know you are a pastor, but God has cast you away from His presence because you refused to forgive brother so-and-so."

I was shocked to discover bitterness and unforgiveness had taken me away from the presence of God. How were my prayers going to be answered? I repented and asked for forgiveness. It was then that I was released from that jail. I understood what it meant to be handed over to the tormentors if you fail to forgive.

In Matthew 18:21, Peter asked Jesus a question. "Lord, how oft shall my brother sin against me, and I forgive him? till seven times?" He said, "If someone insults or offends me in the church, how many times should I forgive him?" Jesus answered and said, "I say not unto thee, Until seven times: but, *Until seventy times seven*" (Matt. 18:22).

Jesus continued to give a parable where a servant who owned his master was forgiven. Yet this same servant failed to forgive someone else who owed him. The result was he was delivered to the tormentors. Jesus ended by saying, "So likewise shall my heavenly Father do also unto you, if ye from your hearts forgive not every one his brother their trespasses" (Matt. 18:35).

If you do not forgive your brethren, you cut yourself off from the mercy of God and expose yourself to dangerous demons. Remember that mercy is one of the main arguments you can advance to make your prayers heard. The Bible is full of cries for mercy. Hebrews 4:16 says,

Let us therefore come boldly unto the throne of grace, that we may *obtain mercy*, and find grace to help in time of need.

3. Your Relationship with the Weak

Whoso stoppeth his ears at the cry of the poor, he also shall cry himself, but shall not be heard (Prov. 21:13).

When you look at the ministry of Jesus, you will realize that He really cared for the poor and weak. No wonder He had a powerful prayer life. Your response to the cry of the weak will determine God's response to your cry.

And when ye spread forth your hands, I will hide mine eyes from you: yea, *when ye make many prayers, I will not hear*: your hands are full of blood. Wash you, make you clean; put away the evil of your doings from before mine eyes; cease to do evil; Learn to do well; seek judgment, relieve the oppressed, judge the fatherless, plead for the widow (Isa. 1:15-17).

When you are ignorant, financially weak, or desperate, it makes you vulnerable, and vulnerable people are usually exploited by the wealthy, knowledgeable, strong, powerful, and rich. For example, when people are sick, you can easily maltreat them; when they are ignorant, you can tell them all kinds of fantastic stories to exploit them financially. Although it will appear to have no consequences, there are spiritual implications. It hinders your prayer life.

That was one of the problems God had with Israel in the days of Isaiah. He accused them of oppressing the vulnerable, like the poor, orphans, and widows. This was the result.

God said, "When you make many prayers, I will hide My eyes from you." Hours of prayer were not going to bring answered prayer because one of the "rules of engagement" had been broken.

We then that are strong ought to bear the infirmities of the *weak*, and not to please ourselves (Rom. 15:1).

The fact that we are in a stronger position does not mean we should exploit the weak. There are men who sexually prey on women who are financially or emotionally vulnerable.

There are also women like Delilah, who exploit men who become emotionally vulnerable to them. I have also seen pastors manipulate and exploit people because of the spiritual control they have over them. All of these hinder the power of your prayer. Remember, your answered prayer hinges on it!

Chapter 4

The Rule of Favour

THE WORD "FAVOUR" MEANS to be kind or partial to someone. It also means to assist or help someone. The favour of God will make God assist you, be kind to you, and be partial to you. Answered prayer is determined by favour.

My Little Girl

I have four children. Sometimes what I do for them partly depends on the level of favour they have in my eyes. The older ones know that their youngest sister has more favour in my eyes because of her age. They also know that sometimes they must meet some obligations before they can get me to give them some favours. Some of these things include cleaning their room, doing their homework, etc.

However, I do not place such responsibilities on my little daughter because she is too young to carry out some of these obligations. She doesn't have to sweep, clean her room, etc. She has favour because she is young and cute. Because of this the rest of my children try to use her to obtain favours from me.

One day I was in my room when she came and said, "Daddy, I want to tell you something."

"Really? What do you want to tell me?" I asked.

She answered, "Can we go to the mall?"

"What are we going to do at the mall?" I enquired.

"We are going to buy pizza and some toys," she replied.

Judging from the conversation, I gathered one of her siblings had sent her.

I looked at her and asked, "Who sent you?"

She looked at me innocently and said, "Caleb sent me."

Caleb is my eldest son and he knows that favour is important if his requests are going to be granted.

In the "rules of engagement," favour is important for answered prayers. What I want you to understand is although God has many children, some of them enjoy more favour than others, and it shows in their prayer life.

Jesus Enjoyed the Favour of God

Jesus enjoyed a lot of favour before God. Because His disciples knew this, they always asked Him to pray on their behalf. When Lazarus died, this is what Martha said about the prayer of Jesus.

In John 11:21-22, Martha said, "Lord, if thou hadst been here, my brother had not died. But *I know, that even now, whatsoever thou wilt ask of God, God will give [it] to thee.*"

Martha said, "You have favour before God that we don't have. I asked God to bring my brother to life, but nothing happened. As for You, I know God will hear Your prayer, because You have favour in His sight."

During the baptism of Jesus, God made it clear that Jesus had more favour than all His children.

Now when all the people were baptized, it came to pass, that Jesus also being baptized, and praying, the heaven was opened, And the Holy Ghost descended in a bodily shape like a dove upon him, and a voice came from heaven, which said, *Thou art my beloved Son; in thee I am well pleased* (Luke 3:21-22).

When all of God's people were baptized, nothing unusual happened. But the minute Jesus stepped into the water, the heavens opened and the Holy Spirit came down. God said, "I have children, but this is my beloved Son, He is special to Me. Not only that, I am also pleased with Him." The level of favour you enjoy in the eyes of God will greatly influence your prayer.

YOU CAN GROW IN FAVOUR

I once employed a certain young man to work for me. He did it with his whole heart and served me very well. The favour he had in my eyes grew because he was very faithful and good to me. It reached a point where I was now ready to help him do anything he wanted to do. He became like my son. How did this happen? He grew in favour.

Did you know that you can grow in favour? Jesus was born with some measure of favour, but He consciously increased the level of favour upon His life.

And the child grew, and waxed strong in spirit, filled with wisdom: and the grace of God was upon him. And Jesus *increased* in wisdom and stature, and in *favour* with God and man (Luke 2: 40, 52).

You can deliberately increase the level of favour you enjoy before God. The more favour you have, the more powerful your prayer life will be.

HOW TO OBTAIN THE FAVOUR OF GOD

I allow my kids to watch TV during the weekends. When they come and ask me for permission to do so, there are certain questions I ask them before I grant them that favour. I may ask questions like, "Have you done your homework?"

"Have you done your quiet time?" "Have you cleaned your room?"

When they answer, "Yes" to any of these questions, they are free to enjoy that favour. Therefore, they know what to do to gain my favour. Because of this, they always make sure they do the things that will win my favour before they ask me for anything. In the same way, there are clear steps you can follow to attract and enjoy the favour of God!

When God decided to give the gold and silver of the Egyptians to Israel, He said to Moses in Exodus 3:21, "And I will give this people *favour in the sight of the Egyptians*: and it shall come to pass, that, when ye go, *ye shall not go empty.*"

Favour prevents a man from going empty-handed when he approaches God in prayer. It prevents you from walking away empty-handed after being in a relationship for seven years. Favour will ensure that your requests are met and your hands are full with the blessings of God and man.

Though we are not born with the favour of God, it is something we can work out. "How?" you may ask. By meeting the conditions. I have good news for you. After reading this book, you will enjoy a high level of favour before God.

HOW TO WIN FAVOUR

He that sent me is with me: the *Father* hath not left me alone; for I *do always* those *things* that *please* him (John 8:29).

I know the things that please my wife and I sometimes do those things to win favours from her. I know what I have to do, especially when night approaches. I know the right buttons to press to gain favour, you know what I mean? Similarly, there are certain things that please God and win His favour.

Jesus said, "I know exactly what to do to win my Father's favour, and I do those things always." Not sometimes, but always.

Do you remember that Saul lost favour before God? He consulted a witch and disobeyed God when He asked him to smite the Amalekites.

So Saul died for his transgression which he committed against the Lord, even against the word of the Lord, which he kept not, and also for *asking counsel of one that had a familiar spirit,* to enquire of it (1 Chron. 10:13).

To attract the favour of God, we must learn to do the things that please Him. What are these things?

1. Holiness

One morning, the Lord spoke to me and said, "When I hanged my Son on the cross, it was My final answer and response to sin. It incurs My greatest displeasure."

Jesus Pleased God Because He Was Holy

Now when all the people were baptized, it came to pass, that Jesus also being baptized, and praying, the heaven was opened, And the Holy Ghost descended in a bodily shape like a dove upon him, and a voice came from heaven, which said, Thou art my beloved Son; in thee I am *well pleased* (Luke 3:21-22).

I ask myself, *What had Jesus done up to this point to win the favour of God?* At this time He had not fasted for forty days, He had not started preaching, and He had not healed or converted anyone, but God was so pleased with Him. What could be the reason? The reason is simple: holiness.

When John the Baptist saw Jesus approaching him for baptism, this is what he said:

Behold the *Lamb of God*, which taketh away the sin of the world. And I knew him not: but he that sent me to baptize with water, the same said unto me, Upon whom thou shalt see the Spirit descending, and remaining on him, the same is he which baptizeth with the Holy Ghost (John 1:29, 33).

Jesus had the nature of the lamb, a symbol of purity and holiness; that was why the Lord was pleased with Him.

Jesus saw Herod spiritually as a *fox*. He said in Luke 13:32, "Go ye, and tell that *fox*, Behold, I cast out devils, and I do cures to day and to morrow, and the third day I shall be perfected." A fox cannot win the favour of God because of its nature.

Many people came to John for baptism, and as he was baptizing them he had visions of their nature. One day John saw some pastors (Pharisees) coming for baptism. God opened his eyes and saw them as snakes in the realm of the spirit. He said, "O generation of *vipers*, who hath warned you to flee from the wrath to come?" (Luke 3:7).

These pastors did not win the favour of God. Rather, they had incurred the wrath of God, although they were in full-time ministry. However, when it was Jesus' turn, God said, "This is my Son; not just any son, but my beloved Son. He is the One I love." Why was it so? Because He was a lamb, "holy!"

There are many religious people who are willfully living in sin yet cry to God in prayer and at all-night meetings. Unfortunately they have substituted holiness for works. Mind you, Jesus had not even fasted for one day when God showed Him favour.

Holiness Secures Answered Prayers

The sacrifice of the wicked [is] an abomination to the *Lord*: but the prayer of the *upright* [is] his *delight* (Prov. 15:8).

I know people who have gone on a twenty-one-day dry fast but have a wife and two girlfriends. I have also seen thieves parading at all-nights, fasting and praying. Though I believe in fasting, I also believe in priorities. Holiness secures more answers than fasting.

Many people have substituted holiness for religion. The word "religion" means what you do for God. They have sown fig leaves to cover their nakedness. They jump from prophet to prophet, man of God to man of God, church to church, and prayer meeting to prayer meeting. Sometimes all of these things are done to camouflage our disobedience. All you need to do is be holy, and when you whisper, heaven will hear.

James spoke about pure religion. He said,

Pure religion and undefiled before God and the Father is this, to visit the fatherless and widows in their affliction, and to keep himself *unspotted* from the world (James 1:27).

Two things are mentioned here: "concern for the poor and the vulnerable," and secondly, "holiness." God enjoys the prayers of a holy man but is angry with the prayer of a wicked man; it does not matter how hard he prays or how many gifts he brings.

The sacrifice of the *wicked* is an *abomination* to the *Lord*: but the prayer of the *upright* is his *delight* (Prov. 15:8).

Behold, the Lord's hand is not shortened, that it cannot save; neither his ear heavy, that it cannot hear: But your *iniquities* have *separated* between you and your God, and your sins have hid his face from you, that he will not hear (Isa. 59:1-2).

THE FEAR OF GOD

He will fulfil the *desire* of them that *fear him*; he also will *hear their cry*, and will save them (Ps. 145:19).

There is a certain realm in prayer where you do not even have to open your mouth; God picks prayer topics from your mind and heart and answers them. This level of favour is, however, available for those who fear God.

Then they that *feared* the *Lord* spake often one to another: and the *Lord harkened*, and heard [it], and a book of remembrance was written before him for them that *feared* the *Lord*, and that thought upon his name (Mal. 3:16).

When you fear God, even your casual conversation becomes like a prayer unto God. I have seen it many times in my own life when something I said in a casual conversation manifested as an answered prayer.

My Faulty Phone Was Replaced

Some time ago I used to have a nice phone which I really liked, but it suddenly developed a problem. That same day while I was in conversation with one of our pastors, I said, "This phone is not good. I have to change it and get a new one."

The following day a brother came to me and said, "Prophet, I just thought I should bring you this gift." When I opened it, it was the latest model of my faulty phone. God had listened to my conversation and responded to my comment.

HOW TO DEVELOP THE FEAR OF GOD

How can you cultivate the fear of God? I believe there are several ways, but I would like to share one with you one.

The *fear of man* bringeth a snare: but whoso putteth his *trust* in the Lord shall be safe (Prov. 29:25).

First of all, I want you to notice two types of fear are contrasted: "the fear of man" and "the fear of God." Secondly, I want you to notice, the word "fear" is substituted for the word "trust." Trust in God is synonymous with the "fear of God." When you trust God, it is the same as fearing God.

WHAT IT MEANS TO TRUST THE LORD

Proverbs 3:5-7 says, *"Trust in the Lord with all thine heart*; and lean not unto thine own understanding. In all thy ways acknowledge him, and he shall direct thy paths. Be not wise in thine own eyes: *fear the Lord*, and depart from evil."*

I want you to notice that again "trust in the Lord" is the same as fearing the Lord. What can you do to develop your trust in the Lord?

Do Not Lean or Rely on Your Head; Rely on Your Heart!

In the story of the twelve spies recorded in the book of Joshua, Caleb and Joshua relied on their hearts whilst the other ten relied on their minds. They could not figure out how they could fight with giants. Because of this they murmured against God and could not make it to the Promised Land.

I remember when I made the decision to go full time into the ministry. The future looked bleak because I was now going to plant a church and there was no guarantee it would work. However, I decided to rely on the word God had given to me that I was called and to trust Him. Second Corinthians 5:7 says we walk by *faith* and not by *sight*.

Lean Not on Your Own Understanding or Depend on Your Mind

Many people are trying to understand God when they are supposed to trust Him. They have questions in their minds, *Why did my mother die? Why did I fail? Why did my wife leave? How can this incurable disease be healed?* etc. Remember, you are supposed to *trust*; not *understand*.

Acknowledge Him in All Your Ways

One definition of the word "acknowledge" is to recognize the authority of someone. When I became born again, I decided to recognize God as the final authority in my life. I sought His counsel through the Word and prayer. By His Spirit I followed His plans for me concerning my work, marriage, and even where I lived.

There were times when I had to deny myself many things in order to listen to my Master. I recognized Him on all my decisions to the best of my knowledge and ability.

He Shall Direct Your Path

Finally, these three steps will culminate in one thing: "He shall direct your path." This means God will be your guide. Once you do this, it will attract the favour of God and it will become the power behind your prayer such that when you pray, things will begin to move because you have won His favour.

Chapter 5

The Rule of Faith

TO WIN THE FAVOUR OF GOD you must be a man of faith because faith pleases God. When all your material needs are met and there is no crisis in your life, it is easy not to exercise faith. With a good, well-paid job that pays your bills and meets all your obligations, you can easily settle in a nice, comfortable church and basically not exercise much faith. But remember, without faith it is impossible to please or win the favour God.

I believe God sometimes allows challenges to come our way because it causes us to exercise faith. Do not forget that you and I were made for His pleasure. I always want to exercise my faith because I want to please God and win His favour. I try to be proactive and look for opportunities to exercise my faith.

A Paralyzed Woman Healed

Recently I was preaching at a conference when I saw a woman lying motionless in front of the stage. When the service was about to end, the Spirit of God said to me, "I am ready to heal that woman if you can believe it."

I said, "Lord, I believe."

Then He said, "Ask what is wrong with her, and after, announce that she will be healed within the next three minutes."

I said, "What is wrong with this woman?"

Another woman came to the front and said, "This woman is my sister and she is paralyzed from head to toe."

The Holy Spirit said to me, "Now tell them she is going to walk and after she is going to dance."

I boldly said it and asked for the woman to be brought to me. I made her relatives prop her up in an upright position and then I held her hand and said to the people supporting her, "Now everyone back off."

The devil said to me, "This woman will fall down and you will disgrace yourself."

I said, "Get thee behind me, Satan."

When they left go of her, the paralyzed woman now stood unaided. I pulled her toward me and started walking with her. At first her steps were short and unsteady, but with each step her gait became firmer and stronger than previously. By the time we reached one end of the stage, I let her go, and she started walking by herself, and finally, she started dancing by herself. Jesus healed her! Faith had won the favour of God.

The People of Israel Failed
to Exercise Faith

Moreover, brethren, I would not that ye should be ignorant, how that all our fathers were under the cloud, and all passed through the sea; And were all baptized unto Moses in the cloud and in the sea; And did all eat the same spiritual meat; And did all drink the same spiritual drink: for they drank of that spiritual Rock that followed them: and that Rock was Christ: But with many of them *God was not well pleased*: for they were *overthrown* in the wilderness (1 Cor. 10:1-5).

God was not happy with the children of Israel because their faith was overthrown in the wilderness. They had problems with water, temptations, and powerful enemies. Unbelief filled their hearts and they started murmuring against God. Because of this they lost the favour of God.

And all the congregation lifted up their voice, and cried; and the people wept that night. And all the children of Israel murmured against Moses and against Aaron: and the whole congregation said unto them, Would God that we had died in the land of Egypt! or would God we had died in this wilderness! And wherefore hath the Lord brought us unto this land, to fall by the sword, that our wives and our children should be a prey?

were it not better for us to return into Egypt? And they said one to another, Let us make a captain, and let us return into Egypt (Num. 14:1-4).

In Numbers 14:28, God said, "Say unto them, [As truly as] I live, saith the *Lord*, as ye have spoken in mine ears, so will I do to you." Why was God angry with them? A lack of faith!

The Wilderness Experience

Every man goes through a wilderness in his lifetime. This is when we face challenges and problems we do not have answers for. When you come to such a season in life, remember it is an opportunity to please God with faith and win His favour.

Do not waste your tears in a wilderness because it offers you an opportunity to please God. As you read, you may be sick, or having problems with one of your kids, or facing a marital challenge. Keep on praying and believing God because it is always better to die in faith than to die in unbelief!

Hebrews 11:13 says, "These all *died in faith*, not having received the promises, but having seen them afar off, and were persuaded of [them], and embraced [them], and confessed that they were strangers and pilgrims on the earth." When you fail to exercise faith in difficult times, the situation will remain unchanged, but faith offers a window of change.

Have you noticed in the Bible that Jesus hardly used money? His primary source of income was faith. Do you want to marry? Exercise faith! Do you want to build a house? Go ahead in faith! Do you want to be in the ministry? Exercise faith, because it wins the favour of God.

We must always believe God for the impossible. I always want to do things that are beyond my natural ability because that is the realm of faith. Let's learn to live above our limitations and resources. We must learn to depend on God in faith for all things.

May you be a man of faith! May you be a woman of faith! In the name of Jesus!

THE WILL OF GOD

In Luke 22:42, Jesus said, "Father, if thou be willing, remove this cup from me: nevertheless *not my will*, but *thine*, be done." One way to win the favour of God is to do His will.

Most firms give bonuses at the end or the beginning of the year. This bonus may vary in size, depending on the level of the employee or the contribution of the employee. When employees follow the "will of the company" and excel in their given area they win the favour of the company and it makes them enjoy a bonus.

The word "will" means the capacity to take decisions. God has left the capacity to make decisions in the hands of every man. When we choose the will of God, it pleases Him and wins His favour.

Jesus said in John 5:30, "I can of mine own self do nothing: as I hear, I judge: and my judgment is just; because I seek not mine own will, but the *will* of the Father which hath sent me." In other words, He said, "I don't make My own decisions. God takes decisions on My behalf."

If you obey the will of God, it will always place you at the centre of God's favour.

Marriage and the Will of God

The choice of a marriage partner is one of the most important and difficult decisions you may ever have to make apart from the decision to serve God. Before I got married I came across many different people I could have married, but I had a silent cry in me that said, "You must let God choose a wife for you."

I prayed, fasted, and committed my way to God. On one occasion there was a friend I was considering marrying, but one day I had a very frightening vision concerning her.

In this vision, I had gone to visit her, but she was tied to a tree in front of her house. She was being guarded by two men, one short and one giant. They told me I should not come to the house again if I did not want any trouble because the girl was their property. The giant was very strong and uprooted trees to display his strength. The short one had great spiritual power; he waved his hand and I started changing into a bird. The metamorphosis started from my feet, then finally, only my head was human. I could not believe it.

At that point I burst out in tongues and suddenly my body started emitting a bright light. This light reversed the process. Then the Spirit spoke to me. He said, "If you marry this lady you will be battling these two spirits for the rest of your life." I discarded the whole idea entirely after I had that vision. It was not God's will and I wanted to please Him.

In Romans 8:28 the Bible says, "And we know that all things work together for good to them that love God, to them who are the called according to [his] purpose." When we follow the purpose, plan, or will of God, all things will work for our good. There are Christians who flout the will of God with impunity yet court His favour.

People flood all-nights and prayer meetings looking for answers to prayers, yet they do not follow God's basic will as revealed in the Scriptures and by His Spirit. I want you to position yourself in the will of God.

My Children Did Not Obey My Will

One day my wife and I went out in the evening. When we came back our kids were still not asleep. They had taken advantage of our absence to go against our will. They were jumping and playing around, knowing full well it was past their bedtime. I was angry and drove them to sleep.

After a while, my little daughter, who always enjoys favour in my eyes, came and said, "Daddy, I want to eat."

I said to her, "You will not eat. Go and sleep."

At that point she had lost favour before me because she had disobeyed my will. Because of that her request was denied. If you go against the will of God, you will lose favour.

Following the Will of God Makes You Bold

And this is the *confidence* that we have in him, that, if we ask any thing according to his will, he heareth us: And if we know that he hear us, whatsoever we ask, we know that we have the petitions that we desired of him (1 John 5:14-15).

When you follow the will of God it will make you bold and confident in prayer. On the other hand, when you live in sin you will be timid in prayer because sin undermines your confidence.

The *righteous* are as *bold* as lions (Prov. 28:1b).

When Adam sinned in the garden, he went into hiding. Disobedience to the will of God made him lose favour before God.

And they heard the voice of the Lord God walking in the garden in the cool of the day: and Adam and his wife *hid* themselves from the presence of the Lord God amongst the trees of the garden. And the Lord God called unto Adam, and said unto him, Where art thou? And he said, I heard thy voice in the garden, and I was *afraid*, because I was naked; and I hid myself (Gen. 3:8-10).

Fear is the enemy of faith, and the mother of fear is disobedience.

I remember when I was in my teens. Any time I went against my dad's will by disobeying him, I became fearful when he came home. I would stay far away from him and would not dare ask him for any favour, like using his car, because I knew I had done something wrong. People who go against the will of God will be fearful and stay far away from Him.

Following the Will of God Guarantees Answered Prayers!

And if we know that he hear us, whatsoever we *ask*, we know that we have the petitions that we desired of him (1 John 5:15).

Our petitions or requests in prayer are met when we follow the will of God.

Do you want your prayers to be heard? Then follow the will of God and watch yourself secure answered prayers.

When we build a life that is centred on the will of God, it creates a fertile ground for answered prayer. A powerful prayer life is more of a life-style than an act.

Chapter 6

The Rule of Mercy

"Daavi," the Food Vendor

BACK IN HIGH SCHOOL we used to buy food from a certain food vendor called Daavi. With time we began to understand and know her better. We learned that all we had to do was to say a few words in her language and we were assured that our helpings would be doubled.

In the same way, when we learn the nature of God our blessings multiply. After walking with God for some time you can tell when He is at work. I can sometimes tell when God is behind certain things that happen in my life.

UNDERSTANDING THE NATURE OF GOD

Any time you are dealing with someone, it is important that you understand and know the person to be able to relate to that person properly. To relate well with your spouse you must be able to understand his or her background, temperament, etc.

For example, if you marry a choleric wife you may have to deal with someone who is forceful and

independent. Once you understand her temperament you can help her channel those qualities
and release her potential. It will be a blessing
to you and your family. On the other hand, this
quality could be the source of contention.

Again, it is important that a wife who marries
a phlegmatic husband understands his nature.
Phlegmatics may be slow at taking decisions and
also at taking the initiative. An understanding
of temperaments will help you relate well to
different kinds of people. Similarly, to relate with
God and have a good a relationship with Him you
must *understand* and *know* Him.

THREE THINGS THAT DO NOT
IMPRESS GOD

Thus saith the *Lord*, Let not the wise [man]
glory in his *wisdom*, neither let the mighty [man]
glory in his *might*, let not the rich [man] glory
in his *riches*: But let him that glorieth glory in
this, that he understandeth and knoweth me,
that I [am] the *Lord* which exercise lovingkindness, judgment, and righteousness, in the earth:
for in these [things] I delight, saith the *Lord* (Jer.
9:23-24).

Jeremiah 9:23 tells us about three things
that do not impress God: *wisdom*, which I equate
to education; *might*, which refers to physical

attributes like athletics, human ability, and physical beauty; and finally, *riches*, or *money*.

Unfortunately, you can have all the degrees in the world and be a thermometer, but it does not impress God. Your beautiful shape does not impress Him. You may be the most skillful sportsman, but it does not impress Him. Neither can your billions of dollars, private yacht ,or island impress Him.

WHAT IMPRESSES GOD?

God is impressed with someone who understands and knows Him. The Lord said to Jeremiah, "If there is something to boast about, boast in the fact that you *understand* and *know* Me."

The Sign—Before I Got Married

One of the things that made me decide to marry was a gift I received from Auntie Elizabeth, the mother of my spiritual father, Bishop Dag Heward-Mills. It was a centre table for a living room.

At that time the decision to marry had not occurred to me. But as soon as I received the gift, I knew it was time to marry because I had never received a gift from anyone that was related to the building of a home. I could have sold it and used the money for something else, but I got the message.

Romans 1:20 says, "For the invisible things of him from the creation of the world are clearly seen, being understood by the things that are made, [even] his eternal power and Godhead; so that they are without excuse." Sometimes natural events have a way of showing the nature of God.

WHO ARE YOU?

And he said, I beseech thee, *shew me thy glory* (Ex. 33:18).

One day Moses asked God a question. He said, "God, can You show me who You are?" Another word for "glory" is nature. When you come before an important person you must ask the right questions and look for the right things.

There are people who visit the homes of important persons only to see what they have: their cars, furniture, etc. They look at the *acts* of the person. The next time you visit someone influential, try and find out: What is the nature of this person? What are the things he does that produces these *acts*? That is more important than finding out what is in his garage.

GOD IS MERCIFUL

And the *Lord* passed by before him, and proclaimed, The *Lord*, The *Lord* God, *merciful* and gracious, longsuffering, and abundant in goodness and truth, Keeping mercy for thousands, forgiving iniquity and transgression and sin, and that will by no means clear [the guilty]; visiting the iniquity of the fathers upon the children, and upon the children's children, unto the third and to the fourth [generation] (Ex. 34: 6-7).

God revealed his nature to Moses. In summary, God told Moses, "I have two sides. I am a *merciful God*, but I am also a *judge*." Paul confirmed this in Romans 11:22 when he said, "Behold therefore the *goodness* and *severity* of God."

You Must Understand That God Is Merciful

An understanding of the mercy of God is very important if you are to have a powerful prayer life. "Why?" you may ask. Because anytime you pray you will have a feeling of inadequacy. A feeling that there is something you were supposed to have done that you did not do. This can undermine your faith and will in turn cause you to lack boldness and faith in prayer.

I have been a Christian for many years, but I still have that feeling sometimes. I had it when I was a baby Christian and I still have it now, although I am a pastor. That feeling never departs; the feeling that I have fallen short of God's glory. This is how Isaiah described it:

All we like sheep have gone astray; we have turned every one to his own way and the Lord hath laid on him the iniquity of us all (Isa. 53:6).

Paul also described it in this way:

For all have sinned, and come short of the glory of God (Rom. 3:23).

Apart from that, the devil is also around to accuse you that you have not prayed, fasted, read the Word, or been holy enough.

And I heard a loud voice saying in heaven, Now is come salvation, and strength, and the kingdom of our God, and the power of his Christ: for the *accuser of our brethren* is cast down, which accused them before our God day and night (Rev. 12:10).

What can take away this feeling of unbelief, inadequacy, and guilt? The knowledge of the nature of God! That God is a merciful God!

For he shall have judgment without mercy, that hath shewed no mercy; and mercy rejoiceth against judgment (James 2:13).

Mercy makes whatever you may have done in the past of no consequence. It is not accounted for. What you get is not as a result of what you have done. It is just based on the nature of God; His mercy!

A Vision Concerning the Mercy of God

One day I had a vision and found myself before the throne of God. A film of someone's life was being played on a large screen. The man in this film was engaged in sinful activities like beating and cheating people, fornicating, lying, drunkenness, etc. I wondered how someone could do all those things in the full view of God. I could not see the face of this bad man, though; I only saw his back.

As the film progressed, I wondered, *Who is this bad man?* Finally the man turned around. Guess who I saw? It was *me*! It reminded me of the words of Isaiah when he was brought before the throne of God.

Then said I, *Woe is me*! for I am undone; because I am a man of unclean lips, and I dwell in the midst of a people of unclean lips: for mine eyes have seen the King, the *Lord* of hosts (Isa. 6:5).

Although I was not physically involved in such things, God was showing me the state of my heart and spirit.

To my surprise the Lord spoke and said, "Promote this man." I did not deserve it because I was a sinful man. The angels lifted me up and sung, "Once you have promoted him, he is promoted."

I thought, *What kind of promotion is this?* It was then I realized I was standing at the throne of grace. I was not only pardoned, but I was also promoted; not because of my works, but because of His mercy. This was truly the mercy of God at work! From that day I became convinced of the mercy of God in a totally different way.

YOUR PERSPECTIVE ABOUT JESUS IS VERY IMPORTANT

The word "perspective" means how you see things. It is important how you see problems. Every problem could be an opportunity depending on how you see it.

When David saw Goliath, he saw an opportunity: a pretty girl, money, and freedom from paying taxes. When the soldiers saw Goliath, they saw their blood on the streets and ran away. How do you see Jesus?

THE GREAT HIGH PRIEST—JESUS

Seeing then that we have *a great high priest*, that is passed into the *heavens, Jesus the Son of*

God, let us hold fast [our] profession. For we have not an high priest which cannot be touched with the feeling of our infirmities; but was in all points *tempted like as we are,* yet without sin. Let us therefore come boldly unto the throne of grace, that we may obtain mercy, and find grace to help in time of need (Heb. 4:14-16).

This Scripture starts with the word "seeing," which also means "perspective." Your perspective of Jesus is very important if you are to relate to Him well in prayer.

He Is Our Lawyer

Our high priest is in heaven, representing us to God. The job of a high priest is like the job of a lawyer. There is no lawyer who goes to court and tries to put his client in jail. A lawyer is there to protect and keep his client out of jail.

Jesus is in heaven, representing us and pleading our case. Therefore it is important to see Jesus as your lawyer, interceding for you—not against you.

The Son of God—He Is Influential

Apart from Him being the high priest, He is also a very influential person in heaven. He is not just an ordinary person; He is the Son of God.

One day a woman who wanted me to pray for her decided to pass her request through my four-year-old daughter. This was because she was finding it difficult to contact me. When my daughter, Chloe, came from school, she said, "Daddy, I want you to pray for my teacher."

"Your teacher? What's wrong with your teacher?" I asked.

She handed me a letter from her teacher; it was a prayer request. I immediately kneeled down and prayed for her teacher.

When we pass our requests through the Son of God, we can be assured God will get the message right there in His "bedroom."

He Has a Strategic Position

Jesus is not only a son; He is also seated at a strategic position: the right hand of God. It is possible to have a son who is estranged from the father, like the prodigal son, but not this one. Jesus had good relations with His Father and He is seated right by Him. Even if He whispers, God will hear it.

He Empathizes with Us

For we have not an high priest which cannot be touched with the feeling of our infirmities;

but was in all points *tempted like as* [*we are*, yet] without sin (Heb. 4:15).

There is a difference between *empathy* and *sympathy*. The word "sympathy" means to show sorrow, grief, or concern to someone. The word "empathy" means to show sorrow, grief, or concern to someone because you have experienced what he or she is going through.

It is always easy to relate to people who have been through your experience because they are more understanding and caring. Novices, on the other hand, may not appreciate and understand your situation.

For example, if you have not tasted alcohol or drunk before, you can easily say, "I do not know why they cannot stop drinking. Drinking is not a temptation." You can easily say that if you have not been in that situation before. If you know what people get from drinking, you will understand why they struggle to break free. However, a former alcoholic who is now a pastor will be less critical and judgmental. Because of his empathy, he will be more merciful.

Jesus was once man. He knows how it feels to be tempted. He knows how it feels to be betrayed, rejected. and hungry.

I Have Been There Before!

I have been a committed unbeliever before. I have been arrested before, fought before, gone to the disco before. When I see people who are struggling to be committed Christians, I empathize with them. Why? Because I have been there before. It is nice to go to the disco and enjoy the music, alcohol, etc. But the problem is the pleasures of sin are for a season, and also it displeases God.

Once you know that God empathizes with you, you have no excuse to remain in sin. This is because, on the flip side, someone has been through what you are going through and repented to serve God.

You may say, "Pastor, you do not understand my problem. It is very unique."

As soon as you think your situation is unique, you have a ticket to misbehave. First Corinthians 10:13 says, "There hath no *temptation taken you but such is common to man*: but God [is] faithful, who will not suffer you to be tempted above that ye are able; but will with the temptation also make a way to escape, that ye may be able to bear [it]."

THE MERCY OF GOD

Let us therefore come boldly unto the throne of grace, that we may obtain mercy, and find grace to help in time of need (Heb. 4:16).

Sometimes when people do not come to church I know they are purging themselves. Some stay at home for two weeks until they feel holy enough to come back to church. They come back only when they feel forgiven. First John 5:13 says, "These things have I written unto you that believe on the name of the Son of God; that ye may know that ye have eternal life, and that ye may believe on the name of the Son of God."

Forgiveness is not a feeling; it is based on the integrity of God's Word. You do not have to feel forgiven; you must know you are forgiven if you have repented and asked for forgiveness.

Jesus sits on a throne of grace, not justice. For example, the kind of seat that you sit on can determine the kind of activity that takes place. We do not sit behind a steering wheel to cook; we sit there to drive. He is not on the throne to judge us; He is there to show us mercy. If you were fornicating last night, or even twenty some minutes ago, the mercy of God can still reach you if you repent sincerely!

Mercy Produces Faith, Confidence, and Boldness

I have realized why some people do not receive healing in a miracle service. They may feel they are not worthy. They feel, *I have not prayed enough; I have not been good enough; I have not been reading my Bible; I have not been attending prayer meetings; I do not pay tithe; I am not a serious Christian; I do not know John 3:16*; and the list goes on.

My Cardinal Key Is the Mercy of God

As a young preacher I used to pray for hours and be anxious anytime I had to preach. As the years have gone by, I have become more relaxed. Why? Because I do not trust in my prayers or fasting or what I know. I trust in the mercy of God! This does not mean I do not pray and fast. I do, but my faith is geared more toward His mercy.

One day I went to preach outside the country. On our way to the service, I told the pastor, "I feel hungry. I need to go back and eat." Afterwards we went into the service and I preached powerfully, with miracles and signs following.

After the service, the pastor asked, "Prophet, I was very surprised when you ate. I thought you would be fasting and praying before you get there."

I turned to him and said, "I do not rely on fasting and prayers as my cardinal key. My cardinal key is the mercy of God."

If you are able to comprehend that God is merciful, your faith will increase because it will not be dependent on anything but the nature of God.

Two Men Went to Pray

Two men went up into the temple to pray; the one a Pharisee, and the other a publican. The Pharisee stood and prayed thus with himself, God, I thank thee, that I am not as other men [are], extortioners, unjust, adulterers, or even as this publican. I fast twice in the week, I give tithes of all that I possess. And the publican, standing afar off, would not lift up so much as [his] eyes unto heaven, but smote upon his breast, saying, God be merciful to me a sinner (Luke 18:10-13).

This Scripture describes the prayers of two men. The first man said, "Lord, You know me. I pay my tithe. I fast twice a week, etc." He thought he was very spiritual. He thought answered prayer was based on works and his spiritual accomplishments.

The other man stood afar off and prayed something like this: "God, You know me; I am a sinner. I have already broken the hearts of two girls. You know that young girls are my weakness. I was the one who was smoking the other day."

He continued and said, "I do not go to church, I have not joined the choir, I do not pay tithe, I do not go for prayer meetings. I am just an ordinary sinner who just found himself in the house of God. The pastor does not know me, but I ask You for one thing: mercy!"

This was the comment Jesus made about their prayer,

I tell you, this man went down to his house *justified* [rather] than the other: for every one that exalteth himself shall be abased; and he that humbleth himself shall be exalted (Luke 18:14).

Why did the sinner have his prayer answered? He understood the nature of God, that God is merciful.

Do you know that you do not even need to be born again to sometimes receive the mercy of God? Many people who were not born again received miracles from Jesus. What healed them was the mercy of God.

First I want to share with you a letter from an unbeliever who was miraculously healed in a miracle service.

Healed of Liver Failure!

Dear Prophet,

My health was retiring and I was sinking daily. I couldn't tell what was wrong.

A colleague in the office told me of the drastic change in my complexion and loss of weight. I was troubled! When I got home that evening, my mum confirmed it. I became more disturbed!

The next day I reported it to our company doctor who asked me to conduct a series of medical tests—*HIV, hepatitis A and B, liver function*, etc. Finally I was diagnosed with liver inflammation. This meant I was losing the enzymes in my liver. My whole life came to a halt. What could I do when I had just been made aware of how close I was to losing my life? The doctor became so concerned. He thought I was too young for that.

He demanded I took a "bed rest." Two days later, you had your conference.

My sister and mum thought the convention was timely. They challenged me to dare *God*. I disobeyed clinical advice and attended the convention.

You asked all sick people to come forward for prayers and I did. When I got home after the convention, I felt relieved. I went jumping and praising the Lord.

Three days after the convention, I mentioned to my doctor that I was healed. He didn't believe it.

He asked me to do further tests at three different laboratories to prove it. I picked up the results and they all proved my liver was all right.

He couldn't believe it and asked me to conduct it again in two weeks. That also confirmed that I was healed.

I have since had a reason to believe in *God* through Jesus Christ the Son!

God healed an unbeliever!

1. The Mad Man of Gadara

And when he was come out of the ship, immediately there met him out of the tombs a man with an unclean spirit, Who had [his] dwelling among the tombs; and no man could bind him, no, not with chains (Mark 5:2-3).

The word "legion" means six thousand (6,000). This man had six thousand demons living in him. He was far from being born again, but Jesus had mercy on him. He was fully possessed, yet he received a miracle. If a fully possessed man can receive a miracle, how much more you?

Jesus told him, "Go home to thy friends, and tell them how great things the Lord hath done for thee, and hath had *compassion* on thee" (Mark 5:19b). I want you to note that the word "compassion" means mercy.

The devil has undermined our confidence, boldness, etc., because he has taken away our faith in the mercy of God. May the mercy of God find you today!

2. Blind Bartimaeus

And it came to pass, that as he was come nigh unto Jericho, a certain blind man sat by the way side begging: And hearing the multitude pass by, he asked what it meant. And they told him, that Jesus of Nazareth passeth by. And he cried, saying, Jesus, [thou] son of David, have mercy on me. And they which went before rebuked him, that he should hold his peace: but he cried so much the more, [Thou] Son of David, have mercy on me. And Jesus stood, and commanded him to be brought unto him: and when he was come near, he asked him, Saying, What wilt thou that I shall do unto thee? And he said, Lord, that I may receive my sight. And Jesus said unto him, Receive thy sight: thy faith hath saved thee (Luke 18:35-42).

When Jesus organized a conference in Jericho, Bartimaeus did not attend it. Instead of seeking first the Kingdom of God, he was busily seeking money in town. He did not give an offering, nor pay tithe, nor join the choir. But as soon he heard that Jesus of Nazareth was by passing, he started shouting, "Lord, have mercy on me!" He just went straight to the point.

Unlike some of us, he did not bother to sing two worship songs before asking for healing. We feel we must do something to earn the mercy of God. Bartimaeus said, "I do not know any song." Let me get to the point. Have mercy on me and give me two brand new eyes." Jesus healed him.

I have not seen any passage in the Bible where people sung worship songs before asking Jesus for healing. I am not saying worship is not helpful, but I am saying God can heal you without a song. Neither did I see Jesus ask anyone if he was born again or a member of a church before praying for him. Jesus operated many times on the basis of mercy.

The time has come for us to be frank in our prayers. It is better you get straight to the point. Lord, have mercy on me. I need a husband and I need one now! The doctor said I have a fibroid, and should consider having a child. Lord, have mercy on me. Have mercy on me, I need a job and I need it now! I need money, and I need it now! I need healing and I need it now! I need a break-through and I need it now! Looord, have mercy on me!

Do you know where that boldness comes from? An understanding of the mercy of God! God will answer your prayers when you appeal to His mercy.

Chapter 7

The Rule of Love

"He Ripped Me Off"

ONE DAY I MET a stranger at an airport and she said, "Prophet, so good to see you. You do not know me, but I have a problem I would like to discuss with you." I decided to give her some of my time.

She continued, "I have this boyfriend who has taken a huge amount of money from me and broken the relationship. Prophet, what do I do?"

"Do you still love him?" I asked.

"Yes, but he has taken my money and I want it back because he did not marry me."

Upon further enquiries, I got to know the money involved was a lot. I asked, "Was it given as a loan?"

She answered, "Yes!"

I asked her why she gave out such a huge amount of money to him.

She replied, "You know, Prophet, I loved him, and so based on that, he started borrowing money from me. I realize he exploited me because he knew I would do anything for him." She continued, "For this reason, he ripped me off."

Because this man knew the love this woman had for him, he capitalized on it to ask for a lot of money and finally ripped her off. Similarly, if you know how much God loves you, you can "rip Him off!"

Thus saith the *Lord*, Let not the wise [man] glory in his wisdom, neither let the mighty [man] glory in his might, let not the rich [man] glory in his riches: But let him that glorieth glory in this, that he understandeth and *knoweth* me, that I [am] the *Lord* which exercises lovingkindness, judgment, and righteousness, in the earth: for in these [things] I delight, saith the *Lord* (Jer. 9:23-24).

He that spared not his own Son, but delivered him up for us all, how shall he not with him also *freely give* us all things? (Rom. 8:32).

An understanding of the love of God will boost your prayer life.

God said to Moses, "If there is an aspect of My nature that you must know and understand, it is this: *I am a loving God*; a God of love!" When your knowledge of the love of God grows, you can pray with confidence and faith.

Delilah knew Samson loved her and that was why she was able to make him tell her the source of his strength. Even when he became aware

Delilah wanted to assassinate him because of previous attempts on his life, his love for her blinded him. What made Samson give his life for Delilah? Love! Love can turn a smart person into a fool.

THE NATURE OF LOVE

Set me *as a seal upon thine heart*, as *a seal upon thine arm*: for *love [is] strong as death*; jealousy [is] cruel as the grave: the coals thereof [are] coals of fire, [which hath a] most vehement flame (Song of Solomon 8:6).

Love Is Tangible

This verse describes the nature of love. When you love someone, you want to make it visible. Love always wants to be worn as a seal on the arm. Therefore it is impossible to say you love someone and not express it tangibly.

One way love is expressed is through words. When a young man falls in love he may tell his girlfriend something like this: "Baby, from the time I was born, I had a question in my heart. But from the day I saw you, girl, for the first time in my life, I saw the answer walking to the question. I love you, girl."

When a girl falls in love with a boy, the name of the boy will creep into every conversation. Even if you are having coffee with her, Esther will say something like, "Andrew does not like this type of coffee." And if you were to ask, "Who is Andrew?" she will tell you all about her newly found love.

Similarly, when we become born again, the new love we have for Christ makes us witness about this Jesus whom we have met. God also makes His love tangible to us by responding to our prayer.

He that spared not his own Son, but delivered him up for us all, how shall he not with him also freely give us all things? (Rom. 8:32).

Healed of a Spinal Problem

Just this afternoon I saw God respond to my prayer in love. A woman with a spinal problem who could not walk was brought to me by her children for prayer. I laid my hands on her and prayed for Jesus to heal her.

Initially nothing happened. But while I was speaking to her children, suddenly the power of God struck and she started vibrating in her chair. Both she and the chair shook. A noise like a gust of wind escaped out of her lips. Suddenly she started shouting, "I am healed! I am healed!" She jumped up from the chair and started walking to the glory of God. The love of God found her and healed her!

Love Is As Strong As Death

The power of love is as strong as the power of death. I remember when my father died. At his funeral, he would not respond to anything. People wept, people called out his name, but he lay motionless.

When people fall deeply in love, they can sometimes behave like dead people. No amount of talking, advice, or counsel can stop them from breaking up a bad relationship. They become "dead in love" and do not respond to any external influence from parents, friends, pastors, and well-meaning people.

When you grasp the depth of God's love, no amount of guilt the devil will throw your way can undermine your faith. May God bless you contrary to people's protestations!

Love Can Make You Give All Your Substance

Love can make you give everything away, including your house. Song of Solomon 8:7 says, "Many waters cannot quench love, neither can the floods drown it: if a man would *give* all the substance of his house for love, it would utterly be contemned."

There was a friend of mine who fell helplessly in love with a certain lady. Within a matter of days he had made the lady a co-owner of his company.

I was shocked! Meanwhile, I had known him for years, but he had never given me anything substantial. What made him do this? It was love!

Because God loves us, He is ready to give everything, including His Son. "For God so *loved* the world, that *he gave* his only begotten Son, that whosoever believeth in him should not perish, but have everlasting life" (John 3:16).

Romans 8:32 says, "He that spared not his own Son, but delivered him up for us all, how shall he not with him also freely give us all things?" God wants to make His love tangible to us. God wants to give us everything, including His Son. What a blessing!

IT IS DIFFICULT TO UNDERSTAND THE LOVE OF GOD

The love of God is difficult to know and understand. Many people know the love of God in theory, but it is something you must know spiritually and experientially. When you know it, it gives you faith and boldness. It gives you the audacity to ask and believe He will do it.

For this cause I bow my knees unto the Father of our Lord Jesus Christ, Of whom the whole family in heaven and earth is named, That he would grant you, according to the riches of his glory, to be strengthened with might by his

Spirit in the inner man; That Christ may dwell in your hearts by faith; that ye, being rooted and grounded in love, May be able to comprehend with all saints what [is] the breadth, and length, and depth, and height; *and to know the love of Christ, which passeth knowledge*, that ye might be filled with all the fulness of God (Eph. 3:14-19).

WE ARE SUSPICIOUS ABOUT THE LOVE OF GOD

And to know the love of Christ, which passeth knowledge, that ye might be filled with all the fulness of God (Eph. 3:19).

Many years ago, whilst walking with a certain young man I knew, we ran into a girl we knew in the neighborhood. My friend invited her to a party he was organizing. This was her reply.

She said, "Ei, Joe, I know you. I think you have evil intentions toward me."

The girl doubted the sincerity of the invitation; she thought the invitation had an ulterior motive.

We usually doubt the love of God and think there must be an ulterior motive when He invites us to serve Him.

When I was an unbeliever, I was told God loved me, but I did not believe it because I thought He wanted to make my life miserable by sending me off as a poor missionary to struggle somewhere. The devil always seeks to misrepresent the love of God.

THE LOVE OF MAN AND THE LOVE OF GOD

There is a certain love God has for us which passes understanding. It cannot be understood or explained. You can only know it by revelation or experience. We unconsciously compare the love of God with *human love*. This makes it difficult for us to appreciate it. One of the basic differences between the love of God and the love of man is human love is *conditional*. We love people for a reason.

Romans 5:6-8 states, "For when we were yet without strength, in due time Christ died for the ungodly. For scarcely for a righteous man will one die: yet peradventure for a good man some would even dare to die. But *God commendeth his love toward us, in that, while we were yet sinners, Christ died for us.*"

Christ did not wait for us to be saved, sing hymns, play the piano, pay tithes, join the choir, or get a degree before dying for us. When we were reeking of alcohol, rejected by a lover, poor, broke, disappointed, and sick, He still loved us enough to die for us.

Jesus said, "Ye have heard that it hath been said, Thou shalt love thy neighbour, and hate thine enemy. But I say unto you, Love your enemies, bless them that curse you, do good to them that hate you, and pray for them which despitefully use you, and persecute you" (Matt. 5:43-44). For this reason we love our neighbours and hate our enemies. Imagine a complete stranger met you on the street and gave you ten thousand dollars as a gift. It would be difficult to receive it because we are used to receiving money in exchange for something. But the love of God is different. Oh what love!

Surely this love cannot be understood. That is why it takes revelation. "To comprehend with all saints what [is] the breadth, and length, and depth, and height; And to know the love of Christ, which passeth knowledge."

The Hardcore Unbeliever

One day I witnessed to a hardcore unbeliever gentleman who gave his life to Christ. The following day I went to visit him and found him in bed with his girlfriend. I took him outside and asked him why he wanted to go back to his old lifestyle.

He looked at me and said, "Last night was a mistake. I don't want to give my life to Christ again!"

I was shocked! That was the first time I ever heard someone say that serving God was a mistake. No amount of words could change his mind.

This gentleman had obviously heard about the love of God but could not comprehend the breadth, depth, length, and height. It comes only by revelation! He valued the love of his girlfriend more than the love of God.

The extent to which you are convinced of someone's love will always determine the kind and type of favours you ask from the person. It is very easy for me to ask my wife for anything because I am convinced she loves me.

THE WHOLE FAMILY IN HEAVEN AND EARTH

For this cause I bow my knees unto the Father of our Lord Jesus Christ, Of whom the *whole family in heaven and earth* is named (Eph. 3:14-15).

I am a twin and have a very strong relationship with my twin brother. I did not come into the world alone; I came with someone. I can ask my twin brother for anything, and as long as it is in his capacity to do it, I am convinced he will.

The strongest relationships on earth are family relationships. Within families there exists a certain level of love and security that transcends any other human relationship. This makes family members able to ask other family members for favours which they dare not ask people outside the family. We must understand that we are part of a spiritual family that spans heaven and earth and transcends blood relations.

I have some family members in the UK, and the distance between us has not abrogated the relationship. Whenever I am travelling, I remember some of my family members and say things like, "Lord, let angels join me in this car and protect us." For the Word says in Psalm 91:11, "For *he shall give his angels charge over thee*, to keep thee in all thy ways." We have a Father in heaven and a certain type of faith. Confidence will be missing when we don't appreciate this fact.

May an angel of God go before you this week! May your family members be around you everywhere you go! May your angels protect you! And may every trap be destroyed, in the name of Jesus!

THE EFFECT OF UNDERSTANDING GOD'S LOVE

Now unto him that is *able to do exceeding abundantly above all* that *we ask or think*, according to the power that worketh in us (Eph. 3:20).

It is only when we have this revelation of the love of God that we can begin to pray for the unimaginable; things that are beyond our thinking and abilities. I believe we move into the zone of the miraculous. Our faith is charged and boldness enters our heart.

The Prodigal Son Understood His Father's Love

Luke 15 talks about the prodigal son. There were two brothers, an older one and a younger one. The younger one understood his father's love and went ahead to ask for his portion of his inheritance.

The elder one did not understand his father's love. This affected his prayer life. He never asked his father for anything so he never got anything. All he did was work.

And he said, A certain man had two sons: And the younger of them said to [his] father, Father, give me the portion of goods that falleth [to me]. And he divided unto them [his] living. And not many days after the younger son gathered all together, and took his journey into a far country, and there wasted his substance with riotous living. And when he had spent all, there arose a mighty famine in that land; and he began to be in want (Luke15:11-14).

After the younger one had squandered all the money given to him, he repented and went back to his father's house. This is how he was received. Luke 15:22-24 says,

But the father said to his servants, Bring forth the best robe, and put [it] on him; and put a ring on his hand, and shoes on [his] feet: And bring hither the fatted calf, and kill [it]; and let us eat, and be merry: For this my son was dead, and is alive again; he was lost, and is found. And they began to be merry.

This was the response of the older brother,

And he answering said to [his] father, Lo, these many years do I serve thee, neither transgressed I at any time thy commandment: and yet thou never gavest me a kid, that I might make merry with my friends: But as soon as this thy son was come, which hath devoured thy living with harlots, thou hast killed for him the fatted calf (Luke 15:29-30).

This lack of understanding of the love of his father affected the prayer life of the older brother. He did not ask for anything.

The store houses of heaven are filled with good things. It can be all yours if only you can deepen your understanding of the love of God.

Someone's breakthrough is lying in heaven right now! Someone's wife is standing in heaven right now! Someone's wedding gown has been sown already in heaven! Someone's car engine has been started by an angel in heaven right now! May you understand the love of God!

LOVE PRODUCES FAITH

For in Jesus Christ neither circumcision availeth any thing, nor uncircumcision; but *faith which worketh by love* (Gal. 5:6).

Love is a fuel that faith needs to work. I remember when I was a student. I had enough faith to sometimes borrow my wife's car because of the love I knew she had for me.

The more understanding you have about how much someone loves you, the more faith you will have toward the person.

I Want a Woman Who Can Spend Money

I once met a gentleman who told me he was looking for a wife.

"What kind of wife are you looking for?" I asked.

He replied, "I am looking for a woman who can spend money."

I was a little amazed, but he was serious.

When I asked him why, he answered, "If I find a woman who likes spending money, it will push me to make more money."

God is looking for someone who knows how to spend the grace of God. May you understand the love of God!

Chapter 8

The Rule of the Name of Jesus

The Epileptic Child

THE NAME OF JESUS IS the key to signs and wonders.

For to do whatsoever thy hand and thy counsel determined before to be done. And now, Lord, behold their threatenings: and grant unto thy servants, that with all boldness they may speak thy word, By stretching forth thine hand to heal; and that *signs and wonders* may be done *by the name of the holy child Jesus* (Acts 4:28-30).

One day a certain woman brought her epileptic child to me for healing. I took a bottle of anointing oil and prayed over him in faith, based on James 5:14-15a, which reads, "Is any sick among you? let him call for the elders of the church; and let them pray over him, anointing him with oil *in the name of the Lord*: and the prayer of faith shall save the sick." This means that the power is generated by the name of Jesus.

After about four months the mother came to see me. She said, "Prophet, from the day you prayed for my son, the epileptic attacks have ceased, and he is completely healed." That is the power behind the name of Jesus!

And he said unto them, Go ye into all the world, and preach the gospel to every creature. He that believeth and is baptized shall be saved; but he that believeth not shall be damned. And these *signs shall follow them that believe; In my name* shall they cast out devils; they shall speak with new tongues; They shall take up serpents; and if they drink any deadly thing, it shall not hurt them; they shall lay hands on the sick, and they shall recover (Mark 16:15-18).

One great distinction between the men of God in the Old Testament and New Testament is in the Old Testament they did not practice the casting out of devils. Neither Elijah nor Elisha cast out devils. The person who formally started deliverance was Jesus.

It Shall Not Harm You

Once a certain doctor told me she had accidentally pricked herself with a needle while operating on someone who had hepatitis and AIDS. She was sad and very disturbed.

I told her, "I know a Scripture that was written purposely for your situation."

"What Scripture is that?" She asked.

I replied, "The Bible says in Mark 16:18, 'And if they drink any deadly thing, it shall not hurt them.'"

I continued, "You will agree with me that not every Scripture applies to you at any given time. However, there are times in your life when particular Scriptures apply to you."

I told her, "We are going to pray based on this Scripture. By the name of Jesus, everything will be okay."

She started to smile.

The name of Jesus worked. It did not affect her.

The Disciples and the Name of Jesus

After these things the Lord appointed other seventy also, and sent them two and two before his face into every city and place, whither he himself would come (Luke 10:1).

Jesus sent His disciples to specific cities to preach and assured them of His presence. I want us to look at the report they returned with.

And the seventy returned again with joy, saying, Lord, *even the devils are subject unto us through thy name* (Luke 10:17).

They said, "When we mentioned the name of Jesus, all the devils in the cities succumbed to us." May demons bow when you mention the name of Jesus! May evil spirits run away when you mention the name of Jesus!

The Demon on Transfer

One day I was invited to preach in a certain church. After the pastor had introduced me, a demon-possessed woman stood up and started shouting.

The demon said, "You! When I was in so-and-so city you tormented me and cast me out and I relocated to this city. Now you have come to this city also to harass me."

Aha! I said to myself, *I think I have met this demon before. This demon must be on transfer.*

I commanded the evil spirit to come out in the name of Jesus. She shrieked with a loud voice, fell on the floor, and started shaking.

After a while she became still and unconscious. She remained in that state until the service was over. She regained consciousness after we had closed the service. There is power in the name of Jesus.

Nothing Happened When I Mentioned the Name of Jesus

Years ago when I was still a baby Christian I saw very few results when I prayed for people in the name of Jesus. This made me very worried. I used to ask myself, *What is wrong with me?*

Meanwhile, when others prayed I saw demons leave and healings, miracles, signs, and wonders occur. I wondered why nothing happened when I in particular mentioned the name of Jesus. It worried me because I had read all of these wonderful Scriptures about the power in the name.

Demons Can Mention the Name of Jesus

I remember once praying together with a group of pastors for a woman suffering from schizophrenia. Whenever the name of Jesus was mentioned, this woman would laugh out loud and repeat the name of Jesus in a mocking voice. I was very disturbed. Later on I discovered some people in the Bible who experienced a similar problem. Acts 19:13-16 says,

Then certain of the vagabond Jews, exorcists, took upon them to call over them which had evil spirits the name of the Lord Jesus, saying, We adjure you by Jesus whom Paul preacheth. And there were seven sons of one Sceva, a Jew, and chief of the priests, which did so. And the evil spirit answered and said, *Jesus I know, and Paul I know; but who are ye?* And the man in whom the evil spirit was leaped on them, and *overcame them*, and prevailed against them, so that they fled out of that house naked and wounded.

The seven sons of Sceva prayed in the name of Jesus but nothing happened. The evil spirit answered and said, *"Jesus I know, and Paul I know; but who are ye?"* In other words, they said, "We have checked our database and cannot find your name. Who are you?" May demons know you! What surprises me is the demon was not afraid to mention the name himself. He said, *"Jesus I know."* The name was only not working on him; he had the boldness to mention the name himself. Something was missing; something was failing to unlock the power in the name of Jesus. The Bible says in Philippians 2:9-11,

Wherefore God also hath highly exalted him, and given him a name which is above every name: That at the name of Jesus every knee should bow, of things in heaven, and things in earth, and things under the earth; and that every tongue should confess that Jesus Christ is Lord, to the glory of God the Father.

What was it that had failed to release the power behind the name of Jesus? From the Scripture and experience I have come to realize that it is possible to mention the name of Jesus and not have any results. I have seen demon-possessed people mention the name of Jesus without any fear.

When Jesus was anointed in Luke 4:34, an evil spirit mentioned His name in the temple. He said, "Let us alone; what have we to do with thee, *thou Jesus of Nazareth?* art thou come to destroy us? I know thee who thou art; the Holy One of God."

The spirit mentioned the name and still remained in the man. He only left when Jesus cast him out. When a gun fails to fire, the problem is not the bullet; the problem must be with the gun.

THE NAME OF JESUS AND ANOTHER SPIRIT

Not every one that saith unto me, Lord, Lord, shall enter into the kingdom of heaven; but he that doeth the will of my Father which is in heaven. Many will say to me in that day, Lord, Lord, have we not *prophesied in thy name?* and in *thy name cast out devils?* And in thy name done many wonderful works? And then will I profess unto them, I never knew you: depart from me, ye that work iniquity (Matt. 7:21-23).

Jesus spoke about powerful ministers of God who will be turned away at the gates of heaven. This will include powerful prophets who prophesied and did wonderful works in His name. It will also include evangelists and apostles who had cast out devils and did many wonderful works. The interesting thing is, although they did all these wonderful things in the name of Jesus, He said He never knew them.

The word "never" means they were never associated with Jesus at any point in time. Translated into Greek, the word "never" is *oudepote*. It means not even at any time.

If Jesus was never associated with them, what power did they use to perform the miracles? If it was not the Holy Spirit, then it must have been another spirit operating under the guise of the name of Jesus.

Paul gave a warning about the probability of such a thing in his letter to the church of Corinth. Second Corinthians 11:4 reads,

For if he that cometh preacheth another Jesus, whom we have not preached, or if ye *receive another spirit*, which ye have not received, or another gospel, which ye have not accepted, ye might well bear with him.

It is possible to preach another Jesus with another gospel and another spirit other than the Holy Spirit.

Not All Signs and Wonders Are Products of the Spirit of God

The charismatic movement is prone to deception because some charismatics tend to believe that once someone performs signs and wonders, then he must be of God. The fact that someone does signs and wonders in the name of Jesus does not mean that the Holy Spirit is behind it.

Jesus said in Matthew 24:5, "For *many shall come in my name,* saying, I am Christ; and shall deceive many." Not in another person's name, but the name of Jesus. And do you know why they will deceive people? Because they will mention the name of Jesus and operate with another spirit.

A Different Spirit Controlled Saul

And it came to pass on the morrow, that the evil spirit from God came upon Saul, and he prophesied in the midst of the house: and David played with his hand, as at other times: and there was a javelin in Saul's hand. And Saul cast the javelin; for he said, I will smite David even to the wall with it. And David avoided out of his presence twice. And Saul was afraid of David, because the Lord was with him, and was departed from Saul (1 Sam. 18:10-12).

It is dangerous to backslide and still move in power because another spirit can replace the vacuum left by the Holy Spirit when He leaves. I have seen men of God live in sin and still operate with power, signs, and wonders.

One backslidden man of God said that the anointing of God upon him doubles when he fornicates. Why did he say that? Because he could still work signs and wonders!

When Saul sinned against God, the Holy Spirit left him, and the Bible says an evil spirit troubled him. The Holy Spirit was replaced by another spirit. He could still prophesy under "the name of God," but it was not the Spirit of God in operation; it was another spirit. He remained king for forty years. Outwardly everything was the same; same king, same position, power, and control, but he was being controlled by another spirit.

CONDITIONS ATTACHED TO THE NAME OF JESUS

One day someone came to ask my permission to use my name concerning something he was doing. I spelled out certain conditions under which he could use my name; otherwise, I was not going to support what he was doing.

I believe the reason we sometimes do not seem to see the power associated with the name of Jesus is because there are several conditions we may have to meet. The same Jesus who said, "In My name shall they cast out devils," also gave several conditions attached to this name.

Ye have not chosen me, but I have chosen you, and ordained you, that ye should go and bring forth fruit, and that your fruit should remain: that *whatsoever ye shall ask of the Father in my name. he may give it you* (John 15:16).

The words "that whatsoever ye shall ask the Father in my name, he will give it to you" makes the use of the name conditional. Jesus spelled out some conditions attached to His name. For example, if I say, "Give me some money so I can give you some milk," it means I will give you milk on condition that you give me some money.

Let us examine some of the conditions in this verse. Three key conditional words must be noted: *chosen, ordained,* and *fruit.* We will be looking at these words in detail.

I would like to put in a word of caution here. I am not saying the name of Jesus cannot work when you are outside the will of God; otherwise even unbelievers cannot be saved because they have to call on the name of Jesus before they can be saved. What I am saying is a powerful, consistent prayer life backed with signs and wonders thrives within a conducive spiritual environment.

THE NAME AND THE WILL OF GOD

The name of Jesus will work on things God has chosen. In other words, it is effective when used in relation with God's "choices, will, plan, and initiative."

The word "initiative" means to take the first step. Otherwise I could pray in the name of Jesus that God should help me steal, but that will obviously not be God's will. Let us examine one instance where the name of Jesus was used with success. One particular example is when Jesus sent out the seventy to preach.

After these things the Lord appointed other seventy also, and *sent them two and two* before his face into every city and place, whither *he himself would come* (Luke 10:1).

This was the report they brought after a successful mission.

And the seventy returned again with joy, saying, Lord, *even the devils are subject unto us through thy name* (Luke 10:17).

The name of Jesus worked because it was the Lord who "chose" what they did. Jesus chose the people to go to the city and how the city was to be evangelized.

When we do things that are in conformity with the choices and plans of God, it makes our prayers effective. The name of Jesus will work powerfully in an environment where the will or choices of God reign supreme.

And this is the confidence that we have in him, that, if we ask any thing according to his will, he heareth us: And if we know that he hear us, whatsoever we ask, we know that we have the petitions that we desired of him (1 John 5:14-15).

The name of Jesus did not work for the seven sons of Sceva because they were outside the will of God. They were not born again; neither were they sent by the Lord. They mentioned the name of Jesus, but it had no effect on the demons.

Then certain of the vagabond Jews, exorcists, took upon them to call over them which had evil spirits the name of the Lord Jesus, saying, We adjure you by Jesus whom Paul preacheth. And there were seven sons of one Sceva, a Jew, and chief of the priests, which did so. And the evil spirit answered and said, Jesus I know, and Paul I know; but who are ye? And the man in whom the evil spirit was leaped on them, and overcame them, and prevailed against them, so that they fled out of that house naked and wounded (Acts 19:13-16).

Your Choices Matter

Jesus made a comment about the right spiritual atmosphere for miracles.

And he that sent me is with me: the Father hath not left me alone; for *I do always those things that please him* (John 8:29).

He said, "The Holy Spirit is always with Me because I make sure I do the things that please God." Not the things that please me, my wife, or my boss, but the things that please Him. In other words, "I follow the will or choices of God for my life."

Jonah Was Not in the Will of God

So the shipmaster came to him, and said unto him, What meanest thou, O sleeper? arise, call upon thy God, if so be that God will think upon us, that we perish not (Jonah 1:6).

In the book of Jonah, God sent Jonah to preach to the people of Nineveh. He disobeyed and instead took a ship to flee to Tarshish. God became angry with him and sent a great storm into the sea. The sailors and Jonah prayed that the storm would stop, but it did not abate. The prayers of Jonah were unanswered because he was outside the will of God. Finally he advised that they throw him into the sea. That was when the storm ceased.

Then said they unto him, What shall we do unto thee, that the sea may be calm unto us? for the sea wrought, and was tempestuous. And he said unto them, Take me up, and cast me forth into the sea; so shall the sea be calm unto you: for I know that for my sake this great tempest is upon you. Nevertheless the men rowed hard to bring it to the land; but they could not: for the sea wrought, and was tempestuous against them. Wherefore they cried unto the Lord, and said, We beseech thee, O Lord, we beseech thee, let us not perish for this man's life, and lay not upon us innocent blood: for thou, O Lord, hast done as it pleased thee. So *they took up Jonah,* and *cast him forth into the sea*: and *the sea ceased from her raging* (Jonah 1:11-15).

I believe that answered prayer is largely driven by the quality of your personal walk with God. If the choices we make in life are largely in conformity with the will of God, as revealed in

Scripture, and the Holy Spirit, it creates a very conducive spiritual environment for the use of the name of Jesus with signs and wonders following.

I want us to look at four major choices that affect the life of every individual. I believe if we are able to surrender our will to God in these areas, it will help us operate in an atmosphere conducive for answered prayer using the name of Jesus.

Let God Choose Who You Marry

In the light of this, it is important to let God choose who you marry. Solomon made the wrong choices concerning his marriage.

But king Solomon loved many strange women, together with the daughter of Pharaoh, women of the Moabites, Ammonites, Edomites, Zidonians, and Hittites: Of the nations concerning which the Lord said unto the children of Israel, Ye shall not go in to them, neither shall they come in unto you: for surely they will turn away your heart after their gods: Solomon clave unto these in love. And he had seven hundred wives, princesses, and three hundred concubines: and his wives turned away his heart. And the Lord was angry with Solomon, because his heart was turned from the Lord God of Israel, which had appeared unto him twice (1 Kings 11:1-3, 9).

Solomon lost the favour of God because he did things contrary to the will of God. The result was the enemies he used to control started rising up against him. When he walked in disobedience of the will of God, it affected things that were not even related to marriage.

And the Lord stirred up an adversary unto Solomon, Hadad the Edomite: he was of the king's seed in Edom (1 Kings 11:14).

Do you know that God can choose a husband for you? You may say, "Christian boys are very boring. I want somebody who is mysterious." Meanwhile that mysterious person is not a Christian. When you choose the things that God has chosen, it creates fertile grounds for effective prayer using the name of Jesus.

Let God Choose Your Job

When God chooses you to be a man of God and you follow your desire to be a pharmacist, it can affect your prayer life. In the story of Jonah, God chose him to preach to the people of Nineveh but he opted to run away to Tarshish. He took a boat to Tarshish, but the Lord sent a great storm into the sea which nearly capsized the boat. In spite of the prayers of the people in the boat the storm continued.

Later the sailors were forced to throw Jonah into the sea and that was when the storm ended. When we do things outside the will of God it can greatly hinder our prayer.

Let God Choose Your Friends

Do you know that God even has to choose your friends? Second Corinthians 6:14 says, "Be ye not *unequally yoked together with unbelievers*: for what fellowship hath righteousness with unrighteousness? and what communion hath light with darkness?" The implications of this choice are spelled out in 2 Corinthians 6:17-18:

Wherefore come out from among them, and be ye separate, saith the Lord, and touch not the unclean thing; and I will receive you, And will be a Father unto you, and ye shall be my sons and daughters, saith the Lord Almighty.

When we allow God to choose our friends, He has promised to be a father to us. The heart of a father is always soft toward his own children.

Let God Choose What You Do with Your Money

Money is one thing that God uses to test our commitment to Him. This is because money is needed to survive in life. If you cannot trust God with your money, how can you trust Him with your life?

If therefore ye have not been faithful in the unrighteous mammon, who will commit to your trust the true *riches*? (Luke 16:11).

We are told that money represents a test as to whether we can handle true riches. I believe that true riches are spiritual things, like the name of Jesus, because Jesus said, "The flesh profiteth nothing." We have a financial responsibility toward the church, family, ourselves, the poor, and in any area where God leads us.

THE NAME AND WHAT GOD HAS ORDAINED

When translated, the literal Greek meaning of the word "ordain" is *to place*. Another English definition of "ordain" is *to appoint*. There are two types of placement or appointment in our relationship with God: a spiritual placement and a physical placement. When we allow God to place us both spiritually and physically, it creates a conducive environment for answered prayer.

SPIRITUAL AND PHYSICAL PLACEMENT

Many years ago I had an experience with God that changed the entire course of my life forever. The Lord appeared to me in a vision and appointed me as a prophet and a teacher. I have seen the name of Jesus work many powerful miracles, signs, and wonders as I have operated within the boundaries of this appointment or calling. I believe physical placement also has a lot to do with answered prayer. You must be properly located in the right city, job, etc., as directed by the Lord.

The Name of Jesus Worked Powerfully for the Seventy

After these things the Lord appointed other seventy also, and sent them two and two before his face into every city and place, whither he himself would come (Luke 10:1).

The seventy Jesus sent out to preach enjoyed great success in ministry. This was because of placement. Spiritually they were well placed because they were chosen by Jesus—not man. Physically they were well placed because He showed them which cities to visit. The result was prayer backed with signs and wonders.

They came back with a report, saying, "Lord, even the devils are subject unto us through thy name" (Luke 10:17b).

What have you been appointed to do? Do it and see your prayer life thrive.

My Own Experience

When I finished my first degree, I went to America with the view to continue with my post-graduate degree. The Lord Jesus appeared to me and asked me to leave because that was not the place He had appointed for me. He also reminded me I was supposed to be in the ministry. I immediately obeyed this vision concerning my physical and spiritual placement.

I wonder what would have happened if I had disobeyed. I believe the Lord would have still been with me, but it would have been difficult to have a very successful prayer life, as I have now, because I would have been operating outside the will of God.

The Example of Paul

And it came to pass, that, when I was come again to Jerusalem, even while I prayed in the temple, I was in a trance; And saw him saying unto me, *Make haste, and get thee quickly out of Jerusalem*: for they will not receive thy testimony concerning me (Acts 22:17-18).

Paul was instructed by the Lord concerning his spiritual placement. He was to leave Jerusalem and preach the Gospel to the Gentiles.

It would not have mattered how hard he would have prayed in the name of Jesus. If Paul had persisted in having his ministry in Jerusalem, he would have borne very little fruit. This is because he would have been operating outside God's placement.

THE NAME AND "FRUIT"

But the fruit of the Spirit is *love, joy, peace, longsuffering, gentleness, goodness, faith, meekness, temperance*: against such there is no law (Gal. 5:22-23).

It is important we bear spiritual fruit if we are to have a powerful prayer life. Jesus said, "You should go and bring forth fruit that whatsoever you may ask the Father in My name, He will give it to you."

I want to break the fruit into two categories: our relationship with others and our relationship with God. This is important because this is closely connected with the law of relationships, which I mentioned earlier. Without a good relationship with God and man, your prayer can be greatly hindered.

1. Fruit and Our Relationship with Others

Therefore if thou bring thy gift to the altar, and there rememberest that thy brother hath ought against thee; Leave there thy gift before the altar, and go thy way; first be reconciled to thy brother, and then come and offer thy gift (Matt. 5:23-24).

Spiritual fruit have to do largely with our *character* and *nature.* We are usually forced to bear this fruit as we relate to other people. Love, longsuffering, gentleness, goodness, and meekness are usually borne in the soil of relationships.

Relationships expose our weaknesses and test our strengths. It forces us to work on the weak areas of our character. For example, marriage requires temperance or self-control. It can force you to control your emotions as you try to build a better relationship with your spouse.

Relationships can test our strength because when you are strong in a particular area, it will take longsuffering and gentleness to deal with people who may not be as intelligent as you are. It is important to bear fruits because one condition of answered prayer is having a harmonious relationship with other people. The development of these fruits helps us meet that requirement.

I believe the reason divorce is on the increase is because we are not longsuffering. This has resulted in many broken homes. "Longsuffering" literally means to suffer for long. The only way to develop it is by suffering for long.

"Meekness," on the other hand, means "being humble to the Word of God." When the Bible says, "Do not commit adultery or fornication," we must be humble enough to obey.

"Temperance" means "self-control." Even when we are angry, we must be able to control ourselves and not hurl swear words and insults.

When you borrow someone's money, be sure to pay it back. These things grieve the Holy Spirit. You should not only bring forth fruit, but your fruit should remain, not just for a week, but for a long time.

2. Fruit and Our Relationship with God

When we relate with God by prayer, the Word, and holiness, we produce the fruit of *love, joy, peace,* and *faith.* The name of Jesus will work when we have *faith.*

In Acts 3:16, the Bible says, "And *his name through faith in his name* hath made this man strong, whom ye see and know: yea, the faith which is by him hath given him this perfect soundness in the presence of you all."

Do you know why demons can mention the name? Because when they mention it, there is no faith behind it. It takes faith to activate the power in the name! Our faith grows as we study God's Word and relate to Him.

For example, when a doctor is performing a surgery, you may think he has just cut a portion of a patient's skin. But in his mind he has opened about ten medical books that you cannot see. That action may look like a simple procedure, but that procedure is based on years of study and experience.

It is the same with prayer. When I am praying, for instance, I just say a few simple words. But in my heart I may have opened many Scriptures in my spirit that you cannot see. You may think it is a simple procedure, but it is a complex one. It is those Scriptures that generate the faith needed to work miracles.

THE NAME OF JESUS AND REVELATION

Ephesians 1:18-21 says,

The eyes of your understanding being enlightened; that ye may know what is the hope of his calling, and what the riches of the glory of his inheritance in the saints, And what is the exceeding greatness of his power to us-ward who believe, according to the working of his mighty power, Which he wrought in Christ, when he raised him from the dead, and set him at his own right hand in the heavenly places. Far above all principality, and power, and might, and dominion, and every name that is named, not only in this world, but also in that which is to come.

Paul prayed for the church in Ephesus to have revelation in three areas: *their calling*; *the riches of His glory*; and *the power of God*. Concerning the power of God, he emphasized that the church would have a revelation about the name of Jesus.

There are different ways you can know things. You can know them intellectually, experientially, or spiritually. Sometimes when we read something from the Scripture, we may know it mentally but not spiritually.

Revelation is understanding and knowing things by your spirit. That was why Jesus said to Simon Peter, "Flesh and blood has not revealed this to you." In other words, you did not know this mentally. When we have a revelation about the name of Jesus, we will have access to the exceeding great power of God.

My Search

Years ago as a young minister I became frustrated by the lack of power, signs, and wonders in my ministry. I embarked on a scriptural and spiritual search to find answers as to why I was not working miracles with the name of Jesus. I bought many books about the name of Jesus. I also used my Bible and concordance to read Scriptures concerning the name of Jesus. At certain periods I combined this with prayer and fasting.

Then one day something happened. I was praying in my room when I was suddenly caught up in the Spirit and saw the heavens open. I saw someone like Jesus descending from the clouds. I also saw many angels clothed in white, singing, "Hail the Lord, hail the Lord." Then I saw Jesus walking in the midst of them. I said, "Jesus is coming." I felt a great power and presence in my room. Then I fell down to worship.

When He came and stood before me, something told me to lift up my head and look at Him. I noticed there was something odd about His clothes; they were not shining. I have seen Jesus before and His garments radiated with light, but this time there was no brilliance. I wondered why.

When I looked at Him, my eyes locked with two green eyes. I immediately knew this was not Jesus. I was looking at Satan, eyeball to eyeball. The devil was standing there.

Second Corinthians 11:14-15 says, "And no marvel; for Satan himself is transformed into an angel of light. Therefore it is no great thing if his ministers also be transformed as the ministers of righteousness; whose end shall be according to their works."

The fear that gripped my heart was unexplainable. Then I screamed, "Jesus!" Suddenly, I heard a loud explosion, "Boooooom!" All of a sudden a bright light flashed in the room. Satan and his angels were blown away by the name of Jesus.

Then the Lord said to me, "My son, you wanted to know about the name of Jesus. Today I have given you a revelation about the power behind that name. When you pray, you will see My name at work."

You don't need to have this same experience to understand and know the power behind the name of Jesus. God will only have to grant you a revelation in your spirit.

It is not everything that a man can teach you. Some things can be taught by God alone. Jesus said to His disciples, "I have yet many things to say unto you, but ye cannot bear them now. Howbeit when he, the Spirit of truth, is come, he will guide you into all truth: for he shall not speak of himself; but whatsoever he shall hear, that shall he speak: and he will shew you things to come" (John 16:12-13). Even Jesus could not teach everything. He said the Holy Spirit will teach you the rest.

I would like you to lift up your hands and pray that God will open the eyes of your understanding and enlighten you about the power in the name of Jesus.

Father, I pray for Your child. I pray You grant Your child a revelation about the name of Jesus. Amen!

Chapter 9

The White Horse

ANY TIME I READ THE BOOK of Revelation, I feel as if I am watching a scene in a Hollywood movie because most of the things look surreal. You know, heaven will be an interesting place to be. We can never get bored because it seems even the image of God is not constant; it changes.

Sometimes Jesus appears as a man with His hair as white as wool and eyes shining with light. In another place you see Him as a lamb that was slain; and the next time you see Him, He is on a horse with swords coming out of His mouth. What excitement!

THE NAMES OF JESUS

And I saw heaven opened, and behold a white horse; and he that sat upon him was called *Faithful* and *True*, and in *righteousness* he doth judge and make war. His eyes were as a flame of fire, and on his head were many crowns; and he had a name written, that no man knew, but he himself. And he was clothed with a vesture dipped in blood: and his name is called The Word of God. And the armies which were in heaven

155

followed him upon white horses, clothed in fine linen, white and clean. And out of his mouth goeth a sharp sword, that with it he should smite the nations: and he shall rule them with a rod of iron: and he treadeth the winepress of the fierceness and wrath of Almighty God. And he hath on his vesture and on his thigh a name written, King Of Kings, And Lord Of Lords (Rev. 19:11-16).

Some of the names of Jesus mentioned in the Scripture above are the *Word of God, King of Kings,* and *Lord of Lords*. Most people have at least two names but some have even more. In the same way Jesus has several names. John called Him the *Word of God*. That is the name Jesus was referred to before His incarnation on earth.

John 1:1 says, "In the beginning was *the Word*, and the Word was with God, and the Word was God. Verse 14 says, "And the Word was made flesh, and dwelt among us, (and we beheld his glory, the glory as of the only begotten of the Father,) full of grace and truth."

WHAT MAKES THE NAME OF JESUS POWERFUL?

The Word of God, also known as *Jesus*, is the one seen sitting on the white horse. I would like you to notice that the name of Jesus is supported by *armies* and *weapons*.

There is an army in heaven that enforces what He, the Word of God, says. For example, the US president may look like any other human being, but make no mistake; behind his words are armies and weapons that can move at his command. When he says, "Attack," behind that word are nuclear bombs, submarines, machine guns, and army personnel. Similarly, the name of Jesus is supported by spiritual armies and weapons!

WHAT DOES IT TAKE TO RELEASE THE ARMY?

And I saw heaven opened, and behold a white horse; and he that sat upon him was called *Faithful* and *True*, and in *righteousness* . . . (Rev. 19:11).

Jesus, who was leading the army, sat on a white horse. He is able to lead this army because of three qualities He possesses: *Faithfulness, Truthfulness*, and *Righteousness*. I believe this has lessons for us to learn. To have the backing army of heaven in prayer, you will need these qualities.

Vision of the White Horse

A brother once shared a supernatural experience he had with me. He was lying on his bed, listening to an audio message I had preached about an encounter I had with Jesus. He began to pray and asked God for a supernatural experience because he had never had one before. Suddenly a white horse appeared at his bedside. The horse spoke and told him he had been sent by the Lord to bring him to heaven in response to his prayer. He was speechless.

When he mounted the horse its colour changed from pure white to grey. He asked the horse, "Why has your colour changed?"

The horse replied, "I portray the holiness of the person who sits on me; I become darker when you are more sinful."

He bowed his head in shame. You need a particular spiritual quality to mount the white horse.

1. FAITHFUL

The word "faithful" means *loyal*. Loyal to whom? To God and His Word! One of the things that tests your loyalty is *time*.

In Matthew 25 the Bible talks about the parable of the talents. In verse 19 it says, "*After a long time* the lord of those servants cometh, and reckoneth with them.*"

This is one of the things that make marriage, for example, difficult; the passage of time.

Short-term relationships are easy to manage because they don't expose you to different seasons of life.

For example, being in a relationship with someone you met six months ago is different from being in that same relationship after ten years of marriage. The person may have changed radically by putting on a lot of weight. The person may be suffering from low sperm count and now cannot have a baby. This new season can challenge the marriage.

Serving God as a student is different from serving God as a married person. Serving God as a rich person is different from serving God as someone who is broke. Because of this, many people find it difficult to be consistent in their walk with God. The seasons expose weaknesses which hitherto were hidden and untested.

Hebrews 3:1-2 says, "Wherefore, holy brethren, partakers of the heavenly calling, consider the Apostle and High Priest of our profession, Christ Jesus; Who was *faithful to him* that appointed him, as also Moses was faithful in all his house."

Do you know what this means? Jesus was sent forth from God to earth as an apostle to represent God and later went to heaven as a high priest to represent us. But whether on earth or in heaven, He was faithful. A change in status, location, and position did not change Him.

I have seen people backslide because of money. Luke 16:11 says, "If therefore ye have *not been faithful* in the unrighteous mammon, who will commit to your trust the true riches?" If you attend every prayer meeting and you are not faithful to God, it can undermine your prayer. The army may not respond. A powerful prayer life is generated by your lifestyle!

Matthew 25:23 states, "*Well done, good and faithful servant*; thou hast been faithful over a few things, I will make thee ruler over many things: enter thou into the joy of thy lord."

Faithfulness changed the status of that servant from a servant to a ruler. When we are faithful to God and His Word, we will rule in prayer.

2. TRUE

The word "true" means *genuine*. You know, it is amazing how things in the natural realm seem to mirror the spirit realm. The natural realm is truly a manifestation of the spiritual. Increasingly it is becoming difficult to distinguish between the real and the fake in this world.

The Fake Dog

Someone once sold a dog to me, which he claimed was an exotic breed. In fact, under normal circumstances I would not have taken that particular man at his word. But because he was introduced to me by a church member I gave him the benefit of the doubt. Later the dog failed to develop all the features associated with that type of dog. Finally I came to the conclusion that it was fake! I called the man and asked him to come for his dog.

In the same manner God is waiting for some Christians to bear the fruit of the Spirit. Unfortunately, over time they have failed to develop the features associated with Christianity. Do you know what that means? They are fake! The time has come for you to be a genuine Christian because the army and weapons behind the name of Jesus respond to people who are true.

3. RIGHTEOUS

The word "righteous" means *holy*. The only thing the devil cannot copy is holiness. He can copy signs, miracles, power, etc.

When Jesus entered the temple in Luke 4:34, the evil spirit said to Him, "I know thee who thou art; the *Holy One of God*." What gave power to His name was holiness. The evil spirit knew that a combination of the name of Jesus and holiness is a dangerous cocktail.

Dear reader, it is not a question of just rushing to every prayer meeting. It is a question of knowing the rules of engagement. Let's be faithful, let's be true, and let's be righteous; and when we pray with the name of Jesus, the armies of heaven will respond to us. May heaven respond to your prayers!

About the Author

Kakra Baiden

MANY YEARS AGO the Lord Jesus Christ appeared in a vision to Kakra Baiden and called him into the ministry as a prophet, teacher, and miracle worker. He is also known as "the walking Bible" for his supernatural ability to preach and teach the Bible from memory.

Pastor Baiden is an architect by profession and serves as a bishop of the Lighthouse Chapel International denomination. He has trained many pastors and planted many churches within the Lighthouse denomination.

Currently he is the senior pastor of the Morning Star Cathedral, Lighthouse Chapel International, Accra. He is a sought-after revivalist and conference speaker.

He is also the president of Airpower, a ministry through which he touches the world through radio and TV broadcasts, books, CDs, videos, the Internet, and international conferences dubbed "The Airpower Conference." He has ministered the Word on every continent and is also the author of the best-selling book, *Squatters*.

Pastor Baiden is married to Lady Rev. Dr. Ewuradwoa Baiden and they have four children.

For additional information on Kakra Baiden's
books and messages (CDs and DVDs),
write to any of these addresses:

US
26219 Halbrook Glen Lane
Katy, TX 77494

UK
32 Tern Road
Hampton, Hargate
Cambridgeshire
Pe78DG

GHANA
P.O. Box SK 1067
Sakumono Estates, Tema
Ghana-West Africa

E-MAIL: info@kakrabaiden.org

WEBSITE: www.kakrabaiden.org

FACEBOOK: www.facebook.com/KakraBaiden

TWITTER: www.twitter.com/ProphetKakraB

CONTACT NUMBERS:
+233 273 437 440 / +233 249 217 272 /
+233 207575215